Ghosts
North Carolina Shores

Micheal Rivers

Schiffer Publishing Ltd

4880 Lower Valley Road, Atglen, Pennsylvania 19310

Published by Schiffer Publishing Ltd.
4880 Lower Valley Road
Atglen, PA 19310
Phone: (610) 593-1777;
Fax: (610) 593-2002
E-mail: Info@schifferbooks.com

For the largest selection of fine reference books on this and related subjects, please visit our web site at:
www.schifferbooks.com
We are always looking for people to write books on new and related subjects. If you have an idea for a book please contact us at the above address.

This book may be purchased from the publisher.
Include $5.00 for shipping.
Please try your bookstore first.
You may write for a free catalog.

In Europe, Schiffer books are distributed by
Bushwood Books
6 Marksbury Ave.
Kew Gardens
Surrey TW9 4JF England
Phone: 44 (0) 20 8392 8585; Fax: 44 (0) 20 8392 9876
E-mail: info@bushwoodbooks.co.uk
Website: www.bushwoodbooks.co.uk

DEDICATION

For
Shack and Gladys

To listen is to learn,
To see is to understand.

CONTENTS

FOREWORD

The Coastal Plains of North Carolina is wonderful land filled with the magic of what makes life worth living. From the white sands of the Outer Banks to the swamps and rivers that run inland, you can almost see the history of the Old North State forming before your eyes. Great battles have been won and lost here since before the Revolutionary War.

As a result of this history, tales of pirates, statesmen, and political intrigue abound throughout the region. Counties featured here from the Coastal Plains include Hertford, Bertie, Northampton, Wilson, Brunswick, Gates, Chowan, Currituck, Wayne, Edgecombe, Hyde, Johnston, and Craven.

North Carolina received its statehood November 21, 1789, but make no mistake — its tales and legends begin long before that time. The legendary pirate Blackbeard lived and plied his trade from these shores. Though pardoned by Governor Eden, he was hunted and killed in the waters of the Outer Banks, and the Hammond House of Beaufort is reputed to be haunted by the ghost of one of his mistresses.

On August 18, 1587, the first European child was born in America on the shores of Roanoke Island; the story of that child, Virginia Dare, is still one of the greatest mysteries in American History.

Visitors to the Coastal Plains find themselves engrossed with the Outer Banks and its waters including the infamous Diamond Shoals. It is here that you will find shipwrecks by the hundreds and tales of the unexpected... *tales of witches, ghosts, and unearthly sounds.*

The term "paranormal" is a relatively new term to most people. In an earlier place and time, ghosts were ghosts and a haunting was caused by a "Haint," which was a reference to a ghost being in residence in the area. To most, a haunting occurred in the dead of night with foul weather, or a full moon, at a certain time of the month.

The following tales are not ordinary ghosts or poltergeists and are not known to the general public. They have been witnessed in both the daytime and nighttime with no particular conditions to make one wary of when it may happen again. It is without rhyme or reason that these spirits make themselves known to mortal man. It is true some ghosts appear to help those in need, but others can frighten those who are unaware and do not possess the depth of understanding about how these things can happen. Psychologists, scientists, and a host of others refuse to acknowledge that there are things in this world that cannot be readily explained away but still exist. Was it the undigested bit of beef...or was it someone trying to communicate from a worldly plane of existence that we do not yet understand?

It is you the reader who must decide what is possible and what is not. It is you the reader who knows what you have seen with your own eyes and heard with your own ears when you were fully awake and your senses keen. Was it a hallucination, or all a vivid dream? There are reputable men and women who we have placed our trust in all matters of our life that have witnessed the paranormal and they are not questioned publicly for their admissions.

Deep within the dark of night, when the moon shines dully upon your window and you stare into infinity, you may find a shadow next to you. As you begin to shiver beneath your blankets from the cold and watch the shadow draw ever closer to your bedside, close your eyes tightly and try to convince yourself it is not real...then comes the icy touch and the whispers of the voice from beyond the grave.

Say what you want, I know what I saw! CCB

Chapter One:

WARTIME GHOSTS

THE SENTRY

(Hertford County)

The American Civil War will forever linger in the minds of Americans as long as we exist. We fought brother against brother and the final resolve was the formation of the greatest nation the world has ever known. The great state of North Carolina held no exemption from participating in the war. In February 1862, the town of Winton, the county seat of Hertford County, fell to Union forces. It was sacked and burned to the ground as Union forces made ready to advance on the remaining strategic points of North Carolina in an effort to quell the power of the Confederacy and take control of their land. The Confederate troops fought hard to retain their freedom and the town was not taken easily. The Union Navy was heavily armed and met with an ambush as they steamed up the mighty Chowan River heading for a landing at Weldon.

Twelve miles northwest of Winton lay the small community of Saint John's. Today, the town covers seventy square miles and remains a rural farming community with a population of 2,042 residents. This peaceful village was not the easy target the Union thought it would be. Thick wooded areas and no less than four creeks — Chapel Branch, Indian creek, Blue Water Branch, and Turkey creek — surround it. Confederate forces held lookouts at all of these locations as well as the old stagecoach roads that ran from Winton to Weldon and Roanoke Rapids. The soldiers of Saint John's and the surrounding area kept Union forces from advancing temporarily, but not without sustaining losses.

Just outside of Saint John's stood a magnificent two-story home that proudly stated the wealth of its owner. Confederate forces utilized the home and its property until Union forces captured the land and held the remaining soldiers as prisoners of war.

Lush fertile farmland and magnificent ancient Oaks that stood proudly against the southern sky surrounded the stately home. The soldiers were adept at utilizing the resources available to them for defending their homes. With little wonder, these huge Oaks became the perfect setting for placing lookouts for the enemy.

Next to the dirt road in the front of the old two-story house was a particularly large Oak tree. A soldier placed in the fork of this tree sat neatly out of sight from anyone advancing from all but one direction. He could easily be seen from the house, but not from the three other directions. If the enemy were sighted in the day, the soldier standing watch would simply signal the watch from the house with a low hand wave. During the night, if the enemy was seen headed for the house or the road south, he would simply light a small group of matches in his cupped hands and watch for the return signal coming from the house. In any case, it was the soldier's duty to keep to his post and act as sniper or give direction on enemy activity if they came under attack.

After the Union Army and Navel forces captured and burned Winton, the advancement of their forces brought more than the heartache of losing the battle. Union soldiers ransacked homes for miles around Winton, taking livestock, such as pigs and horses, and breaking down split railed fences, using them for firewood. General Sherman's forces had even taken their dignity.

This ancient Oak was reputed to be the tree where a Confederate soldier stood guard watching the main road. He was shot and killed by Union forces trying to take the road west of St. John's. It is said that he still haunts the area around the tree.

In March 1862, Union forces attempted making their advancement through Saint John's and on into Murfreesboro. This proved to be a large mistake! The Confederate soldiers had already prepared for their advance all the way up the Chowan and Tar rivers.

The Confederate sentry, neatly hidden in the fork of the spreading Oak tree, spotted the Union soldiers long before they came within sight of Saint John's and signaled the other soldiers. Immediately, troops massed and prepared for the ensuing battle. The sentry, of course, had no knowledge that a scouting party had

been sent before the main body of Union troops. How the scouting party was able to get so close to Saint John's without being seen is still unknown. The troops came within a half-mile of the house when, without warning, a single shot rang out from the wooded area southeast of the farmhouse. The Sentry fell from the fork of the tree, killed by a single bullet from a Union sharpshooter. With this death-dealing blow, the battle began and the northern troops were held off and rerouted.

The Ghost

There came a day when the war was over, and life returned to normal in this community. Children played and laughed beneath the summer sun. Families rebuilt their homes and returned to normal living. The war was just a bad memory with few reminders, but what about the Sentry?

The sentry's name has passed with time, but the sentry himself refuses to be forgotten. A young farmer from a neighboring town was traveling down the dusty dirt road late one afternoon. He intended to trade or sell his produce and chickens at the general store and be on his way home the following morning. With the sale of these items, he could also buy necessary items such as salt, sugar, and some cloth for his wife to make new clothes for the family. This means of barter was not uncommon for times such as these. He approached the ancient Oak standing close to the road and saw the head of what appeared to be a man wearing an old soldier's cap up in the fork of the tree. The farmer nodded politely to the man, and the man nodded back. When the farmer reached within a few feet past the tree, he looked up into the fork and saw nothing. The tree was barren of leaves; therefore, there was nowhere to hide. He also knew the man could not have come down from the tree without being seen. Shaking his head, he continued on to the general store. A chill raced down his spine when he thought of the man in the tree, but he couldn't explain why.

After attending to his business at the general store, the men sat talking and catching up with all the latest news. The farmer mentioned the man he saw at the old Oak tree. The store owner's face paled slightly and thought for a moment before he answered. While the other men sat quietly, the store owner told the farmer the story of the Sentry. When he had finished, he looked at the farmer and told him, "Now and again somebody comes along and sees him up in the tree. You might be well off not to talk about it. It scares the children."

Years have passed by, and still the sightings have continued. There are no special weather conditions or time of night or day he will appear. A flare of light has been seen coming from the fork of the tree in the dead of night. A few have told of passing the old Oak and seeing a man dressed in grey lying at the foot of the tree. When they approach the tree to assist the man on the ground, he dissolves right before their eyes.

Should you visit the site of this tragedy and feel the experience of a cold chill or see a man from another time, remember…this Sentry is still at his post.

Another Kind of Haunting

Directly across the road from this farm sits a small frame wood house. It once belonged to the main farm, but was sold in later years for a rental house. One of the families that rented the house said that seeing a small light coming from the fork of the old Oak was not uncommon. Their family and visitors have been stirred from their sleep by a moaning sound emanating from where the edge of the old road once existed. This was the same spot where the young soldier lost his life.

This family also explained that even as late as the 1960s the shackles used to hold the slaves at night were still attached to the walls of the basement, and that they heard the chains of the slaves being moved in the night.

COMING HOME

(Northampton County)

Tucked neatly between the towns of Rich Square in Northampton County and St. Johns are many farms and modest homes of the modern south. This land was blessed with rich natural farmlands and natural beauty. Indians indigenous to North Carolina lived and prospered here just as the European settlers did when they first came to North Carolina. On the northeastern border of Northampton County lies the Meherrin River, which is named after a Native American tribe that inhabited the lands long before the settlers came to North America.

This county's infamy goes back long before 1782 and deals with such famous men as Andrew Jackson. The county was also involved in the now famous Nat Turner slave insurrection. The woodlands cast its cooling shade and undeniable beauty along the roadside for all to see and enjoy. In its time, the farms were the main stay of the surrounding towns and communities. The town of Ahoskie in Hertford County was fast becoming the manufacturing capital for the area with Northampton a close second. Ahoskie was also the largest town within easy traveling distance.

The Barmer family resided between the towns of Rich Square and St. Johns, share-cropping a modest farm for its owner. The meager living they subsisted on did not deter them from living a good life. They had food on their table and their mother usually made their clothing. Life was simple and they all worked very hard.

During the days of spring and summer, the family sat through the cool of the late afternoon and evenings on their front porch talking of the day's events or just enjoying friends who stopped by to chat. In many cases, their homes were located far from the main road. To visit, one would have to travel the half-mile dirt lane across a narrow wooden bridge and then another fifty or so feet to the house.

Jim Barmer was Cherokee, adopted by a white family when he was eleven. He believed highly in the spirit of man, living or dead. Strong in his beliefs, he taught his children the things he had learned from his own people in an effort to teach his family respect for all things. Among these ideals was respect for the spirits that walked alongside the living.

In the spring of 1900, the Barmer family had moved into a new home and was enjoying their newfound blessings. It was said long after Jim died that he never wore a shirt or a pair of shoes in his life. It was later found he wore shoes only once. There was three feet of snow on the ground at the time! Jim was given to a no-nonsense attitude toward life and it reflected in every way.

On the first summer evening in their new home, the family was gathered on the front porch talking with friends. The children played in the front yard as the adults entertained themselves with stories of old and what was happening in the community. Earlier in the day everyone had attended church and filled themselves with the Holy Spirit, as the old folks say. Mrs. Barmer had fixed a wonderful supper and the friends all brought a dish of food so they may all dine together. This was a tradition for many southern families. In several areas of Eastern North Carolina, the tradition has never been broken, especially among the Southern Baptist.

The late afternoon sun was still shining brightly upon them. It was at this time a visitor at the Barmer home stopped in the middle of his story and stared down the lane that ran to the house. An uncomfortable silence fell among the people sitting on the porch. Seemingly without reason, the children stopped playing in the yard and turned their attention to the stranger walking up the lane.

He walked steadily and purposely toward the house, never faltering in his stride. They watched him drawing ever closer and were eventually able to distinguish his clothing. He wore the uniform of a Confederate soldier. When he neared the bridge, he looked up and everyone could see his face as he broke into a big smile. Jim began to notice the horses in the yard were twitching and stamping their feet. They tossed their heads nervously. When the soldier reached the little wooden bridge, he deftly laid his hand upon the rail. He waved and smiled, yet the moment his foot settled onto the bridge... *he vanished before their eyes.*

Everyone, including Jim, sat speechless, not knowing what to say. Mrs. Barmer and the other mothers called the children to the house and made them sit on the porch. Jim and several of the men walked to the bridge and found nothing. There wasn't a footprint to be seen or any sign of someone having been there. They only saw the tracks from the horses and carriages that had passed earlier in the day.

Throughout the summer, every evening about the same time, the soldier would appear making his way to the house up the lane. He always smiled, he always waved, and without fail he would vanish when his foot settled on the bridge. The soldier never appeared during the spring or the winter. He was only seen during the cool of the evening in the months of summer.

When the soldier first appeared, there was never a feeling of unease or tension among the witnesses, only the farm animals. It is often said that animals can sense and see things that mortals can't. As the sightings continued, even the family dog began to howl and whine whenever he approached the bridge. Within a few short weeks, the family dog was nowhere to be found. It was Jim's opinion that the old hound had seen enough of the soldier and left of his own accord. The soldier still appeared to be friendly, and yet the feelings held deep within were changing for the worst each time he made his short journey to the bridge. The feelings bordered on sadness and fear of the unknown.

Jim and the family became accustomed to seeing the soldier and accepted him as best as they possibly could. The economics of the time also dictated that a house as nice as this one could not be given up so easily only for the sake of an apparition that never harmed anyone.

The old house has been torn down, but the wooden bridge still stands. The identity of the soldier was never discovered, but time marches on and the soldier's appearance has never been forgotten. Does he still haunt the wooden bridge? There are those who say yes. Other people who know the story of the old soldier are prone to staying away from the area when the warm sun of summer rests upon their shoulders.

THE BATTLE OF BENTONVILLE

(Johnston County)

Three days in March 1865 — the 19th to the 21st — were very possibly the biggest days in the history of North Carolina. It was at this time that the last full-scale action of the Civil War was fought between General Joseph Johnston and General William T. Sherman in Bentonville. It was also the largest battle ever fought in the state.

To visit the battlefield today, one will instantly try to picture how the battle was fought in their minds. Facing the battlefield you can easily spot the artillery ramparts at the edge of the woods. You can almost smell the gunpowder as the cannons fired round after round at the attacking troops while soldiers' rifles echoed around them. The screams of wounded and dying soldiers from both sides haunt the very soul of apathetic visitors who come here. There are 360 soldiers buried on this battleground and a beautiful marker honoring them is placed where it's believed a mass grave is located.

To your left, you can see the museum that houses memories of the Civil War and just beyond it is the Harper House. Built in 1850, this was the home of John and Amy Harper. Their home was captured on the first day of battle and used for the care of wounded soldiers on both sides. General Sherman struck a bargain with John Harper: if Harper agreed to let him use his house, he and Amy would be allowed to stay.

With that, the bottom floor of the house was used for the care of the wounded and the top floor became the residence for John, his wife, and seven of his children. This was a small area to house nine people, but they endured. The balcony at the front of the house on the second floor looks out onto the battlefield. The kitchen is located about thirty feet from the main house as a safety precaution against fire. Everything here has been kept as close as possible to its actual conditions during the Civil War.

People of all ages and walks of life have come to visit the battlefield and to see the Harper house. They have an avid interest or curiosity in the way people lived and, most of all, where they died. For years visitors have reported seeing "actors" at the Harper house.

One spring morning, an eight-year-old girl went to the second floor ahead of her parents and returned minutes later smiling and laughing. When her parents asked her what she was laughing about, she quickly told them about the old bearded man upstairs on the balcony. She said he was dressed in old clothes and made her feel funny inside. The tour guide overheard the conversation and knew no one was supposed to be upstairs at this time and the balcony had been roped off for safety reasons. She was also aware that there were no actors scheduled for appearances at the house. The tour guide quickly excused herself and ran up the stairway, but found nobody there. She was the only person there and nowhere for anyone to hide. At the end of the tour, she asked the little girl to describe the man she saw. The child turned to an antique photograph inside the museum and pointed to the picture of John Harper!

Over the years guides as well as employees have seen and heard things that could not be readily explained. Reports from tourists have also included sightings of Amy Harper in the house.

Reenactment or Time Warp?

In the early 1990s, two couples and their families were visiting while on vacation. The first was a young couple from Georgia traveling with their young son. The other happened to be from Connecticut and they were on their way to the beach with their two children. As fate would have it, they pulled into the parking area of the Bentonville Battlegrounds behind each other, parking nearly side by side.

The children were excited to see a part of American history and eager to roam the field for treasures unknown. Before anyone could move, they began seeing Confederate soldiers coming from the woods and to their left Union soldiers were charging for battle. Smoke filled the air as the cannons roared into action and the soldiers fought and died. Screams filled their ears as the wounded fell where they stood. The cavalry charged the field with a vengeance, shooting men as they appeared to run them down. It was a grand spectacle for the children. When the battle ended, the men went back into the woods, taking their fallen comrades with them.

The parents applauded the show. In their words, it was the finest and most life-like reenactment they had ever seen. They could not wait to develop the pictures they had taken. The two families left the battlefield parking lot and walked over to the Bentonville museum. The smiling lady standing behind the cash register greeted them. She welcomed them and told them about the activities, such as a short film, and many maps explaining the area that was available to them.

All around them they saw the uniforms, swords, guns, and accessories of the soldiers of the Civil War. One of the young gentlemen turned to the lady attending the register and commented on how good the re-enactors were at today's battle. At once she held a puzzled look upon her face and knew he was mistaken; she immediately thought he had meant the re-enactment in March. She told him there were no actors today, but a reenactment was scheduled for March of the following year. She explained the last one held was in March, two months before. He disagreed with her instantly and told her of the battle they had just witnessed minutes before. Before he was able to finish, the young man and his family from Georgia intervened. He told her his family watched it also. Both parties questioned her and said there was no doubt they had witnessed the battle and wondered how she could not have heard the cannons fire as close as the museum is to the battlefield. This was a first for those who worked at the battlefield and has not been heard of happening again. It was an affair that made the local papers and local television reports. Is it possible the soldiers returned to fight a battle from beyond the grave? Most would say no, and the witnesses were very good at raising a tall tale. The pictures they had taken of the battle produced only the loneliness of the battle ramparts lining the edge of the woods.

Both of the families in this story had never met each other before. There was no coordinated meeting or plan to produce an outlandish story for the press. Still, both families witnessed the *same* battle at the same time along with their children. God bless the warriors... May they rest in peace.

GUNNER

(Dare County)

The Virginia Dare Mystery...

Roanoke Island is located at the end of the Virginia Dare Memorial Bridge. As you travel the length of this bridge, you are crossing American history itself. The beautiful blue waters of the Croatan Sound glitter in the morning sunlight just as it did hundreds of years ago when the first English settlers stood upon this shoreline gazing toward the ocean. One mile from this point the first English child was born in the United States. Shortly after, she was to make history with her disappearance. The vanishing of Virginia Dare and the other English residents of the island remains a mystery that may well never be solved. The only clue to their demise was a single word carved into a tree, "CROATOAN."

In the center of the town of Manteo, sites are dedicated to Virginia Dare and the other settlers who disappeared without a trace. She and her fellow Englishmen were not the only people to disappear.

Many people over time have tried to claim heritage to the Croatan Indians, but were never able to. The colonists had once been reported living close to the Chief Powhattan in Virginia. A search by John Smith in 1607 never brought forth any evidence of their being in the Chesapeake, Virginia, area. Nonetheless, the search for any evidence of the colonist or descendants of Virginia Dare continues to this day.

A Lone Sailor...

Roanoke Island residents are a hardy people who have weathered the storms of the Outer Banks for generations. Their linage is long and in some cases distinguished in their own way. They fish from the waters surrounding the island making their living, as well as just enjoying the everyday life on this island of mystery.

The Great American Civil War brought heartache to these islanders and those who lived inland. Ships came and went through the

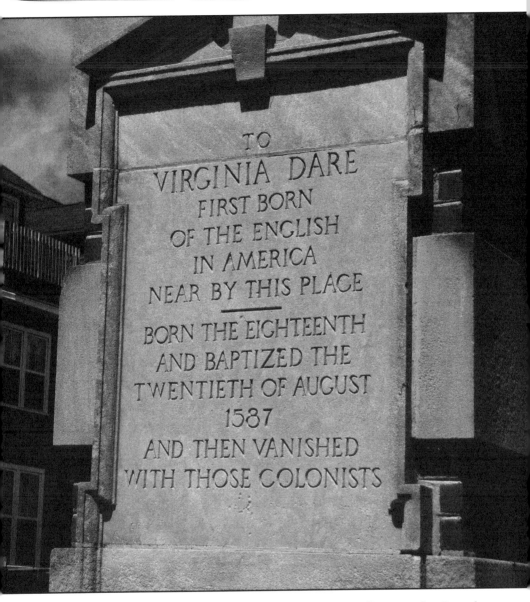

TO
VIRGINIA DARE
FIRST BORN
OF THE ENGLISH
IN AMERICA
NEAR BY THIS PLACE
———
BORN THE EIGHTEENTH
AND BAPTIZED THE
TWENTIETH OF AUGUST
1587
AND THEN VANISHED
WITH THOSE COLONISTS

This monument is dedicated to Virginia Dare and the colonists who disappeared on Roanoke Island. It is located in the center of downtown Manteo by the water's edge.

waters of the Croatan Sound carrying their cargoes of food, clothing, and ammunition to continue the fight that had begun in the War Between the States. British ships supplied Confederate troops with rifles and other supplies to continue life against the opposing forces. On the western shore of Roanoke Island stands a reminder of those days gone past. A sign was erected in remembrance of soldiers and sailors who fought the Northern troops from these shores. They stood valiantly against incredible odds from the Union forces that came to dominate their lives.

One hundred yards south of this sign formerly stood the Confederate base, Fort Huger. To visit this area of white sand and sunshine today is still a sobering moment. Men stood their ground against everyone in this place with little to fight with, but fight they did! Fort Huger was a principle Confederate fort, guarding the Croatan Sound with its cannon placements aimed at any ship or boat not belonging to the cause of the Confederacy. It saw action on more than one occasion and, as war tells its tales, men died. In February of 1862, Fort Huger made history — her cannons were in place, her men readied for action, and the war lay before them like an albatross about their necks.

Life in a fort as small as Huger was not easy. During the summer, the sun beating down on the soldiers and sailors manning the fort could be brutal. The summer nights proved to be a bit cooler, but mosquitoes and sand fleas posed another problem for the men. Then came the winter months and hurricanes. Taking refuge from a major storm here came to be another problem the generals had not anticipated when stationing troops on the island. Soldiers of the Confederacy wore uniforms made of wool, making life miserable for those involved in the war. Fresh water was supplied by wells dug around Roanoke Island and sometimes had to be hauled by horse and wagon to the fort. Their food came by British ships and blockade runners manned by the islanders. This too was hauled to their location by horse and wagon from ports and hideaways along the Outer Banks.

A tale began to surface in the early 1940s about a Confederate sailor who had been seen at the ruins of Fort Huger. The story was taken with a grain of salt, along with many other tales that became popular with the villagers. It was not out of the norm for many to stay quiet about things they had seen that were not of this world. This left the tale to circulate little by little until a great many knew of the sailor. Many days visitors, as well as local children, have been to the old gun placements and played in the sun. At times someone would tell of feeling like he or she was being watched. They

FORT HUGER

Principal Confederate fort on Roanoke Island. Mounted twelve guns. Surrendered Feb. 8, 1862. Earthworks are 100 yards south.

This sign, located at the end of the Virginia Dare Memorial Bridge, was erected by the state of North Carolina for the site of Fort Huger. The site for the fort is one hundred yards south of this sign.

could not explain their feeling, as they knew there was nobody near them to make them feel this way. The low scrub trees seemed to whisper in the wind, adding to this feeling of not being alone on the shore.

Through time people sat upon the shore and fished the waters of the Croatan Sound at night catching Croakers, Spot, and Flounder to their hearts delight. When the moon shone brightly in the southern skies over the island, a kaleidoscope of stars gave the island a look and feel of another place and time... This was usually the time when people *saw* the Confederate sailor standing on the shoreline watching the waves lap against the beach. He stood tall and lean with his head pointed at the horizon. He seemed to be looking toward the open waters in expectation of someone coming. In his hand, he held an old cannon bore swab as if leaning on it for support. Some say it was a bore swab; others claim it to be a heavy staff of Ironwood. In either case, he stands as a heavy

The area formerly known as Fort Huger.

mist against the trees of the island. He turns slowly, yet his face is not distinguishable even in the bright light of the full moon. His appearance to mortal man is not one of a pleasant nature. People who have seen this specter speak of feelings of hatred and a longing to be elsewhere. The red stripes of his shirt stand out boldly as well as the suspenders holding his trousers in check. The dark

trousers begin to fade until there is nothing to see but the beach itself from his thighs down. This was the general description given of the sailor seen standing on the shore.

An Unexpected Sighting...

Richard and two of his closest friends came together on a spring day in 1970. It would not be long before the three of them would be parted from each other for a very long time. His closest friend had joined the Marine Corps and was to leave them by June 27. His other friend was to marry and had planned to move to Alaska to work on the new pipeline. None of these young men knew what life would bring for them after this day.

With the excitement that only the young can muster, the men decided to take one more fishing trip before they had to buckle down to life as an adult. With little conviction and even less money, they pooled their resources and grabbed their fishing and camping gear. They decided to fish the waters of the Croatan Sound by the foot of the bridge of Roanoke Island. They knew the waters by the old fort was one of the best spots they would be able to find with little or no chance of tourist interference. The three of them had fished and played here since they were children and knew the area well.

With enough food and supplies to last them for two days, they piled into Richard's mustang and drove to Roanoke Island, arriving in time to watch the sun as it lightened the beach. They unpacked their gear and traveled a little over a hundred yards south of the parking lot just out of sight of the main road. It was to be a joyous time and good friends together forever. Camp was set up and looking as well as could be expected for these three adventurers.

Nearby they had collected driftwood for a good fire that evening and felt they had everything a man could possibly want. It was time for a swim until the changing of the tide. The tide change would then bring in the fish so they could try their luck at catching supper. They laughed when Richard mentioned the ghost of the old fort. The other boys threw sand at him and told him the story was "a load of crap cooked up to scare the tourists."

Richard felt the story was not just a tale, and yet he wondered what it was like to see something of that nature. A ghost sighting is like the ultimate adventure. Richard questioned them: What if it was true? What would they do if they saw him standing right before their eyes? It was his bet they all would run for the car. Little did they know they were soon to find out what their reaction would truly be.

As the sun started to set, the fishing venture began. They sat on the beach with rod and reel in hand fishing for anything that would bite. They seemed to have more fun talking and daydreaming about days to come than actually catching fish. The moon rode full and high in the clear night sky. Stars shone down on them, as the world about them seemed to be in perfect harmony.

Soon they were catching fish regularly and had the cooler half full by just after midnight. Richard sat perched on a long piece of driftwood. He suggested they stop for the night and build a campfire. Everyone agreed heartily and headed for the campsite.

The fire burned brightly and warmed their chilled bodies. They were tired from the trip and their bellies were swelled from the fish they had consumed with more than just a normal appetite. They laughed about everything and everybody until the conversation died to almost nothing. They lay and studied the stars above them. To these three young men, there was nothing as beautiful in this world as this sky on this night. The breeze flowing across them from the waters made life seem like a wonderful dream.

Sleep overcame the three young men and they lay snuggled deep within the warmth of their sleeping bags. The sound of the waves lapping steadily against the shore was a comforting sound to their ears. At or about 3 a.m. Richard awoke with a start. He looked around him and saw his friends were still sleeping like babies. He had no idea what woke him after only a couple hours of sleep. Sitting up, he looked all around him for anything that could have caused him to wake up and found nothing. Curling up, he buried himself deeper into the sleeping bag and tried to go back to sleep. Sleep was not to come again for him, not on this night. Nearly an hour passed and he decided to get up and walk down toward the beach. The night air was refreshing and yet he had a slight chill that dwelled deep into his bones.

A wave of apprehension struck him as solidly as someone striking him when he neared the water's edge. Minutes passed and the feeling increased. Richard stared out onto the beach questioning why he would feel this way. Not wanting to be alone, he returned to the camp and woke his friends. He told them what had happened and the three of them decided to stay awake and talk for awhile.

They returned to the beach and sat in the darkness, leaning against pieces of driftwood and speaking in low tones. An overwhelming feeling of depression and loneliness seemed to cover them like a blanket...so much so that they did not try to hide it from each other. As Richard turned to his closest friend to say something, he saw the figure of a man walking toward them. Richard pointed toward the man and told his friends someone was coming toward them.

The three young men jumped to their feet and watched the man coming closer with each step. Just as the boys had decided they might run from this man, he stopped within twenty yards of them. They watched as he stood by the water's edge with his head turned toward the far end of the island. He wore a shirt with red stripes and a single solid color suspender attached to a wide belt. In his hand was a pole about five feet in length and what appeared to be a large swab at the end. The man stood leaning on this staff just staring at what appeared to be nothing.

All of their senses began to tingle. Realization had come to them that the form before them was not a man of skin and bone like themselves. From just below his knees to the white sands of the beach there were no legs or feet to be seen. The specter paid no attention to them or anything they said. He just stood and stared out over the water.

The longer the specter stayed by the water, the more the three boys wanted to flee, but they couldn't! Their escape route was blocked by

On this spot Richard and two companions witnessed an apparition defined as a sailor from the Civil War era standing looking out across the water.

a ghost from another time. They watched his every movement no matter how slight, mesmerized by this creature from beyond the grave. What seemed to be hours was in reality just a few minutes of their time. Soon the creature turned his sightless eyes toward them and faded into the mist as if he had never been.

The warm sea breeze touched their young faces once more, awakening them from a sight they would never forget. The feeling they had experienced earlier was gone except for the memory of it all. With a touch of sadness in their hearts, they packed their camping gear and walked slowly back up the beach and found their car. Within minutes, they were on the road crossing the bridge for the trip home.

Truth is Stranger than Fiction...

The three of them never explained truthfully why they ended their fishing trip so soon, but there were some who suspected the truth when they were told the location of their campsite. Months went by and the topic of the ghost was never breached, but they all knew and respected each other for leaving the dead to search for his own peace by the beachhead.

The years ticked away and they all had wives and families of their own. The three of them once again met for old times sake. They picnicked together and reminisced about all the good times they had together. It was not without mixed feelings that the subject of the ghost was brought to light again. At first they had little to say, but that soon changed and they gave their families the entire full story concerning the last camping trip they ever had together. They described in detail what they had seen; the look upon their faces and the tone of their voices gave the listeners cause to believe every word they said. It was their story and a part of a time when they were inseparable from each other.

I know the story well and, yes, I believe it to be true. This area is now privately owned and visitors are not allowed to see the site of the old fort from the land. Camping is no longer permitted with a wooden fence placed in the area to keep visitors away. You can approach the site of the old fort from the water side if you wish to see where the cannons were placed at the time of the Civil War. During the night, if you approach the site of the old Fort Huger, who knows... you may have a ghostly companion to stand with you through the night.

Chapter Two:

NIGHTTIME GHOSTS

BILLIARDS AFTER MIDNIGHT

(Wilson County)

John Miller was born and raised on a farm near Wilson, North Carolina. He was a young man who had just barely become his own man. He found employment in the heart of Wilson and had no car to take him to work. To be closer to his job and ensure he would be able to get there on time, he rented a room in the upstairs of the old Cherry Hotel.

The Cherry Hotel in its heyday was the gathering point for anyone who wanted to turn themselves loose and have a good time. They had a very large bar with dancing and live music. In the back of the building, there was a billiard room where a lot of money changed hands betting on their own or others' expertise with a pool cue. People came from all around just for the large stake poker games. On Saturday nights, a sure bet was the regular appearance of the Wilson Police Department as the result of brawlings, stabbings, and the inevitable gunshot wound. Public intoxication and prostitution were as common as changing your clothes. Blacks, whites, the middle class, and the poor all came to the Cherry Hotel. Strangers from out of town who got themselves a room for the night sometimes wished they hadn't.

The Cherry Hotel was not always this way. When it first opened its doors, it was the finest hotel in the city and catered to nothing but the best. Its restaurant gained the reputation of the best food anywhere in the east. However, by the end of World War II, it had fallen from grace and began to sink into disrepair. That was when the trouble from all sides began to assemble at its doors.

John was able to rent his room for a very reasonable price. It included all of his bedding and towels exchanged daily and free breakfast except on weekends. He lived there for seven months before he was told the Cherry Hotel was closing their doors and he would have to find a room elsewhere.

John felt himself lucky when he was able to find a room for rent in the huge two-story house located next to the hotel. This room was three times the size of the room he had formerly rented and cheaper in price. Over a period of time John had become good friends with the owner of the Cherry Hotel and one evening after work they sat drinking beer and talking. Before long John struck a deal to purchase one of the billiard tables at a very good price. The next day John and the hotel owner, along with two of his coworkers, moved the table into his room on the second floor of the old house.

What was once the Cherry Hotel still stands strong and proud after a great renovation. After its initial closing, many of its furnishings were sold to the public. It now serves as private apartments.

After work he would stop by a local store and buy beer to take home with him. Many evenings friends came by to shoot pool with him and everyone had a good time. A few months after the purchase of the table, John started having trouble sleeping. Getting to sleep was not the problem — staying asleep and getting his rest was a different matter. In the beginning, he thought he was dreaming of hearing the billiard balls clack against each other, moving about the table. He would open his eyes, sit up in bed, and see that each and every ball was just as he had left it.

The sounds continued to escalate. It started out one or two nights a week before turning into a nightly ordeal. John was not prone to superstition or fear. Neither was he a drunkard or mentally unstable. He had never been known to hallucinate and had never been sick enough to see a doctor but once in his life.

The time had come to put the matter to rest once and for all. He had to find the source behind what was happening in his room. He set the alarm on his clock for 1 a.m. and sat up for the rest of the night. John did not have to wait very long. He sat straight up in his bed smoking a cigarette and saw to his amazement the door to his room open. He could see *through* this door to the real door, which was still closed tightly. A tall thin black man about sixty years of age or more walked into the room. He stepped over to the wall to his right and removed his hat. He did not seem to notice John in the slightest. He continued on to hang the hat on a hook that didn't exist. Slowly, with eyes that saw nothing, he reached over and pulled a cue stick from the rack on the wall and inspected it to assure himself it was straight and true. His next move was to walk over to the table and chalk the cue just as if he was about to play the game of his life. The black man carefully racked the balls and played his game for almost half an hour.

John could not believe his eyes. He sat in bed in fear of moving, praying the ghost would not notice him. At the end of the game, the black man turned back and hung the cue stick neatly in the rack, placed his hat upon his head, and left the room. During the game, John could hear each and every billiard ball as they struck each other and moved across the table to neatly drop into the pockets. When the black man had gone, John could see that all of the billiard balls were just as he had left them.

The next morning he awoke early and headed out for work. The more he went over in his mind what had occurred the night before, the more he came to the conclusion that it had all been a strange dream. Chuckling softly to himself, John swore to lay off beer forever.

Once again it came time for John to lay himself down and get some sleep before it was time to get up and go to work again. This was not meant to be. A few minutes past 1 a.m., he was awakened by the sound of feet shuffling across the floor of his room. He opened his eyes and watched as the old black man repeated his previous night's performance exactly. Afraid to move, he waited until the old man left and then jumped from his bed. Not stopping to dress, he left his room and ran down the stairs and into the street. He spent the rest of the night at a nearby bus stop.

John told his friends what had happened and the laughter was such he felt truly embarrassed. Nevertheless, he told them he would give the table to the first man to move it, but it had to be out that evening or he would throw it into the street. His best friend brought a truck around that afternoon and moved the table into his own home. Two days later John saw his friend and asked him if he liked the table. The friend said that while he truly did like the pool table, he didn't have it any longer. His friend quietly told him, "After the first night in my house, my wife made me take the table out back and burn it."

Articles of furniture, clothing, and other items of normal use often bring with them the energy of those who were the owners or felt a love for the items. When you inherit something that may seem trivial to you, stop and think of the love or affection that may have been lavished upon it by someone else. When this is said and done, don't be surprised if the owner decides to admire it once again from beyond the grave.

SHIPPING AFTER MIDNIGHT

(Wilson County)

The manufacturing facilities in the state of North Carolina have been producing goods and services worldwide since before the American Revolutionary War. The variety and quality of these goods are excellent and the demand for them grow each year. One of the Coastal Plains' manufacturers produces high quality discount coupons for retailers, and Mr. Sykes worked for this company for thirteen years before deciding that he could no longer stay in their employment.

Mr. Sykes was a shipping clerk who worked third shift and at the time he was there he was quite satisfied with the company and everyone he worked with. His benefit package was more than adequate as well as his rate of pay, but the time came when no amount of pay or benefits could convince him to stay. When Mr. Sykes began working his shift, he met another gentleman on the first night that he would be working with as long as he was there. They got along well and even fished together on some weekends. They fast became the best of friends.

Just after midnight one November evening Mr. Sykes and his co-worker took their lunch break and then enjoyed a cigarette on the loading dock. During the course of the evening his companion had been telling him that he was planning on putting in his retirement papers within the next few weeks. This was sad news for Mr. Sykes and yet he was glad for him. He had earned the retirement and wished him all the best. They vowed they would still go fishing together and visit often.

Within the hour after they talked, his companion suddenly slumped to the floor in the shipping room, dropping a box of products and spilling its contents. Mr. Sykes went around the end set of conveyer rollers and found him lying on the floor gasping for breath. Mr. Sykes leaned him against a post to try and make him comfortable while he dialed 911. Within minutes, the ambulance arrived, but it was too late. His longtime friend had died before they could reach the nearest hospital.

Months passed and Mr. Sykes worked his nightshift as always, but with a new man to take his partner's place. While the job was still enjoyable, it was not the same without his friend. The holidays were approaching quickly and business was booming. Mr. Sykes was getting all the overtime he could handle. Checking his calendar he thought about the date. It was December 3rd, twenty-two days until Christmas and he would have two weeks off for his seniority. He stopped stock-still and listened. He was sure he had heard someone close by, and yet he saw no one. He looked toward the Ward Room doors on the other side of the rollers. He knew what he was seeing and yet he could not believe his eyes. Passing by the last set of rollers and going through the swinging doors he saw his deceased partner. He was dressed as he usually would have been if he had been working: dark blue trousers with a dark blue shirt. Mr. Sykes broke into a cold sweat after seeing the apparition. He pulled his handkerchief from his pocket and wiped the sweat from his face. Still unsure of his senses, he went back to work, but he was never the same again.

This building is the site of a man who haunted the shipping area long after he had passed. Today the building stands empty due to a poor economy. No sightings of the apparition have been reported in recent years.

When he returned home the following morning, his wife knew something had happened and questioned him about it. He told her the story and she listened, wide-eyed, to his tale. It was her advice that he not tell anyone what he had seen for fear of reprisal from his employer.

Mr. Sykes returned to work and never told anyone what he had witnessed, but it was far from over. Returning from his Christmas vacation, he never gave the ghostly sighting another thought as he went about his duties. The hours rolled by and close to 2 a.m. he thought he heard boxes being moved on the loading dock behind them. Nobody was scheduled to be there until 6 o'clock and the dock was off limits to all but himself and his co-worker. Mr. Sykes went through the swinging doors and out onto the docks. He could not see where anything had been moved and yet he was certain he had heard the noises. The young man working with him said he had also heard the sounds, but he also didn't see anybody come through the shipping room. The sounds continued at different times throughout the next week. Mr. Sykes was beginning to wonder if his old friend had come back and was continuing his work. He laughed to himself and thought about how foolish he was being.

Several months passed without incident until Mr. Sykes walked into the men's room after lunch. His lunch had not agreed with him and he was forced to use the toilet. As he sat there, a strange sensation suddenly rushed through him like an icy chill. He heard the restroom door open and close, but no footsteps were heard. He could see through the crack that was between the door of the stall and the wall itself. There were three mirrors and he would be able to catch a glimpse of anyone coming into the room. Looking straight ahead of him, he suddenly saw the face of his old friend looking into one of the mirrors. Mr. Sykes could have sworn the smile on his face was directed at him. Without hesitation, he removed himself from the seat and ran from the restroom. Returning to his work, he found it difficult to concentrate on his job. He looked around and found that he was alone for the moment. This is where he was mistaken! A voice from the grave came from just over his shoulder calling his name. Mr. Sykes left the shipping area and went to find his new partner. He refused to be alone for the rest of the night.

Over a period of time, others began to see and hear things that were out of the norm. Mr. Sykes, however, decided that he had enough and handed in his resignation. His supervisor tried to persuade him to stay and offered to transfer him to another department. It was all but too late and Mr. Sykes found employment elsewhere.

Should you ever find yourself in this position, just remember…the dead will not hurt you and sometimes a good job is really hard to find.

WALKING AFTER MIDNIGHT

(Edgecombe County)

In the beginning, it was a very pleasant place to call home. There was a little country store almost next door and a few miles down the road was the Tar River. This made it very convenient for a woman who loved her days and evenings spent fishing. There was basically no historical value attached to the land and certainly nothing exceptional had ever happened there. Yet the home and the land gave Mary Ann an odd sensation when she least expected it. The old tobacco barn close to the back of her home was a perfect place to park her new car. She parked it beneath its shed the first day she had the car, but could not explain why she never parked it there again after that.

Mary Ann had purchased this home two years before moving into it. She stayed with her mother and father and rented the home out to friends until she was ready to leave her parents' home. She found a good job in the city of Rocky Mount and realized she was only seven miles from work, so she would save a lot of money in expenses. It all seemed like such a blessing.

A few weeks after she moved in, a few friends came to visit. The evening was perfect for a barbecue and a few drinks with old friends. Just after midnight everyone said there goodbyes and she found herself alone in the house and very happy with her decision to get out on her own. Mary Ann rolled over in her bed and snuggled deeper under the sheets, smiling to herself. Life was good.

A few moments later, she heard footsteps in the hallway headed toward her bedroom. She thought she was alone. Mary Ann was sure everyone had gone home and she had locked the doors, and yet the footsteps drew ever nearer to her bedroom door. With the moonlight streaming through the windows, she could see the door clearly and her heart filled with dread at the prospect of a stranger being in her house with no way to protect herself. Just as she opened her mouth to scream, the footsteps stopped. There was nothing there in her doorway. Gathering all her wits about her and what little courage she had left, she jumped from her bed and turned on her lights. There was no one in the hallway! Calling out in a strained voice, she asked if someone was there. She received only the sound of her own voice ringing in her ears. Carefully she made her way to the kitchen only to find nothing. Checking the doors she found them all still locked and bolted from the inside. Mary Ann breathed a sigh of relief and laughed aloud: "Maybe I drank more than I thought."

The words had hardly passed her lips when she heard the footsteps returning from the bedroom doorway back to the entrance of the kitchen. All the lights were on and there was not a soul in the house but Mary Ann and the *unseen* visitor walking toward her. She shivered from the sudden cold and felt near to falling from the weakness in her limbs. Suddenly the footsteps became silent. Mary Ann sat down on the kitchen floor in disbelief, still wary from what she had just witnessed.

The next day, still shaken from the night before, she returned to her parents home and told her father what had happened. Her father, a gentle man and one never to dispute her word, could give her no answers. He advised her to just put the incident out of her mind and go on with her life. This she tried to do. Later that night the experience happened again. She was not as unnerved as before, but fearful nonetheless. Each and every night at the same time the footsteps traveled down her hallway and back again. Leaving the lights on did nothing to deter the nightly visitor.

Mary Ann's best friend decided to investigate the area for her hoping to find a solution to her problem. The nearest neighbor was more than a half-mile from her home. This gave the possibility of sound travel of her neighbor walking almost impossible. There was no record that anyone had ever died on the property or was in a car accident close by. Her friend exhausted all possibilities without finding any answers.

The footsteps continued nightly and she became accustomed to the sound. There was a point in time when she completely ignored them and slept soundly, but then things started to change. The changes came gradually, but with clarity. Mary Ann arose to get dressed for work one morning and glimpsed a man in farmers' clothing standing by her kitchen table. When she turned to get a good look at him, he was gone. She was sure she had seen the figure and still her mind could not accept what she had seen. Shrugging the incident off, she got dressed for work and left her home.

Later in the day she and some friends talked about her unearthly houseguest. They decided they would experiment a little. That night she and two other friends tied a string of cola cans across the hallway to see what would happen. Shortly after midnight the footsteps sounded in the hallway. They started at the end of the hallway and made their way to the bedroom door as always and stopped. Soon after they retreated back down the hallway and disappeared. The cans never rattled or even so much as quivered as the spirit made his nightly walk. Other experiments were tried and failed. They could not coerce the ghost to make any kind of speech or sound other than his heavy boots in the hallway. Mary Ann still glimpsed him once in a while, but never long enough to see his face. Eventually she moved from her home and sold it to someone she did not know. She never disclosed to them the nightly visitation and she never heard as to whether or not they experienced anything out of the normal.

There are professionals that say a person can be haunted as well as a structure. Mary Ann's mother believed it was she who was haunted and not the house. Mary Ann had never experienced such a thing before and has not been bothered by anything from another plane since. The house is now a private residence and visitors are not welcome. Perhaps they have had a visitor that they do not wish to discuss with anyone.

Chapter Three:

THEIR SPIRIT REMAINS

THE CHAIR

(Bertie County)

Lewiston, North Carolina, a small community comprised of a mere 638 residents in 2000, is easily accessible from Highway 13 North. The residents here enjoy fishing, hunting, and each other's company. During the week nights and weekends, you could find the younger people parked beside the road having their own little party and a few laughs before dispersing, only to meet up again later in the night. Stories abound among these young people and nothing goes unnoticed when something happens in the community.

In the late 1970s, a young girl and her handsome suitor decided to marry. It was a happy occasion for everyone, and her friends were quick to give their approval. David had graduated high school and was fortunate enough to land a good paying job with a local electrical contractor. The charming and beautiful bride, Lottie, gained employment at a local factory. The happy day came and went with all of their friends and relatives at the wedding to wish them well. It seemed to be the perfect union. The first year of the marriage went very well. David's parents had asked them to live with them until they could financially support themselves and buy a nice home nearby.

It was true David's parents looked at Lottie like the daughter they had always prayed for, but were unable to have. She appreciated this and their treatment of her could not have been better.

The old man who lived in this home never left his front porch; he was known for rocking in his chair and waving to passersby. Former residents claimed the chair on the front porch rocked on its own accord and the sounds of footsteps haunted other areas of the old house.

Yet there comes a time when a young woman and her new husband need a home of their own. The privacy alone is worth its weight in gold. She desired all the things a young woman could dream of: furniture of her own, a yard to plant her flowers, and a kitchen to cook for her husband set up just for her.

David worked hard and saved every penny he was able, but by the end of the year it did not seem like a very large amount. His parents kept finding reasons for them not to move and this made their decision all the more difficult when the time came to get out on their own.

Lottie and David finally decided that instead of waiting to have enough of a down payment for a house, they would find something available for rent. However, the small communities surrounding them had little to offer.

Lottie's uncle knew of an old man who had lived almost three miles outside of Lewiston. He had recently passed away and his children were planning on making the old farmhouse available for rent by the end of spring, the uncle told Lottie and David. Both of them knew the house well. Though it sat just off the road, it was still close enough that anyone on the porch could be seen easily. Each day, whenever either of them passed the house, the old man sat in his rocking chair and waved to everyone passing by. He was well known for sitting in his rocking chair and waving at passersby since Lottie and David were just children.

The old man's family came and repainted the house inside and out. They replaced the floor coverings and installed new cabinets as well as updating the bathroom. It was not a fancy house. It was a standard clapboard farmhouse with a pleasant front porch and a swing attached. The living room was small and the two bedrooms were roomy, but had no closets. No trees were in the yard and still the house was fairly cool even in the hard heat of summer. The rain falling steadily on the tin roof would lull you to sleep at night. The house had no air conditioning and a kerosene heater was used to keep warm in the winter.

None of this mattered to Lottie and David. They saw it as an opportunity to have a home of their own and, with this said, they signed a one-year lease. Lottie and David bought what furniture they could afford and the gifts from the bridal shower filled the kitchen and bath. Within a week of signing the lease, they had moved into their new home. They were truly happy!

The days passed without a hitch. The bills were paid on time, friends came by to visit, and Sunday dinner was always at hers or David's parent's house. One Sunday evening after they had returned home, David sat in the rocking chair on the front porch while Lottie sat in the swing. Looking down, David asked Lottie, "Have you ever noticed this front porch?"

Lottie chuckled. "No. Why do you ask?"

David pointed at the floorboards beneath the rockers. "The old man rocked here so much he actually wore grooves into the boards."

Lottie looked down and agreed with him. She tried to visualize how long someone would have had to sit in the chair to create grooves that deep.

In the week to come, David came in from work late one evening. He told Lottie he would have to be gone for a week to attend a school his boss had assigned him to in Greenville, North Carolina. This was fine for Lottie. She knew it would be good for their future and she was not afraid to be home alone. Lottie decided she would take the vacation time she had coming to her while David was in school. David kissed his wife goodbye and left for school on the following Monday.

Lottie cleaned the small house and decided to sit on the porch for awhile. It was a beautiful day and not to be wasted sitting inside by the television. She got a cold glass of ice tea from the refrigerator and sat down in the old rocking chair on the porch. She laughed aloud as she thought of the old man. To her surprise, she almost waved at several passing cars. She sat for about a half hour and then got up to get something to eat. While standing in the kitchen, she heard a creaking sound coming from the front porch. Lottie went to see who was there. She found no one there, but the rocking chair was *rocking* on its own power. She placed her hand on the back of the chair and it stopped its motion immediately. Thinking nothing of it, she returned to the kitchen to have her snack.

The rest of the day was uneventful other than her best friend stopping by for a visit. They sat and talked by the light of the television when both of them heard a sound coming from the front porch. Lottie's friend exclaimed, "The rocking chair is rocking by itself!"

Lottie told her the same thing had happened earlier in the day also. Her friend placed her hand on the chair and it ceased rocking immediately. They both agreed it had to have been the wind that rocked the chair.

On several occasions Lottie would hear the sound of the old man's rocking chair rocking by itself. Yet when she went to look the chair was as still as a mouse. It seemed that any time she was at the back of the house near the kitchen she would begin to hear the sound of the rocking chair moving on its own accord.

The following days were uneventful. The chair did not rock and the house was as quiet as a mouse.

David had been back at home for nearly a week when strange things began to happen again, as he had seen and heard the chair rocking by itself. He had even tried moving the chair out of the grooves only to find the chair back in its original place shortly after being moved.

In the following weeks, Lottie and David's happiness turned into a world of sleeplessness and despair. All through the day and night the chair would rock and creak, sending its sound through the small house like thunder in the distance. Each time they came out to cease the rocker, it was no longer moving. Footsteps echoed in the stillness making their way from the front of the house to the kitchen. It was not unusual to hear the sound of the front screen door opening and closing by itself. There were times when they sat in the living room next to the screen door as it made the sounds of opening and closing...yet it *never* moved! They began to find things missing only to turn up elsewhere in the house. The young couple was at their wits' end and no one would believe them.

The final straw for the both of them came early on a winter's night. They had gone to bed to try and catch up on some sleep. At eleven o'clock they were awakened from a sound sleep and looked toward the foot of the bed. An unidentifiable form stood at their feet and a chill they could not possibly describe penetrated their bodies. They watched as the covers on the bed were slowly being drawn from their bodies and dropped on the floor at the end of the bed. After what seemed to them to be a lifetime, David was finally able to gain his nerve. Grabbing Lottie, he literally dragged her from the bed and they both escaped through the bathroom window. At first light, David went back into the house to gather all their clothing and never returned.

Lottie and David now reside in Manteo, North Carolina, with their two children. He never went back to Lewiston or anywhere near the house he and Lottie once lived. The house has since been torn down to make way for a new commercial development.

UNCLE JOHN'S SPIRIT

(Hertford County)

When the spirit of a man or woman comes to those in the dead of night, it can be a startling experience. Sightings in the light of day are also not out of the norm — it's usually an event that will stand in the memory of witnesses forever. The small community of Dean's Crossroad stands quietly in the furthest corner of Hertford County. This was the home of Council Barmer. He grew up the son of a sharecropper with high morals, and not prone to telling tales that were untrue. The punishment for such a crime would leave you unable to sit comfortably for quite some time.

The summer of his tenth birthday Council and his two brothers and sister had a visitor. Uncle John was not their father's brother. He was actually his father's uncle. Yet, the entire family referred to him as Uncle John. Council was a very large boy for his age and quite often he worked in the fields next to his father, much like a grown man would have done. He had worked with Uncle John on many occasions feeding his livestock and chickens before everything changed. Even at this early age, he and his brother trapped for furs and pelts for extra money, as Uncle John and his father had taught him.

The springtime came with all the wonders of nature surrounding them. The traditions of the older families were always the same. The doors were never locked and at this time of the year the front door and back were left open to draw the wonderful fresh breezes throughout the house. The tempting smells of his mother's cooking wafted in the air, making everyone's mouth water. This was a happy time for all. Yet, there is a fact of life we must all consider at one point in time — a man cannot live forever, and as was the case, Uncle John became gravely ill.

Council's mother was standing by the wood stove in the kitchen preparing the mid-day meal when she heard a knock at the back door. As she turned, a tall slim black man who worked for Uncle John removed his hat and held it before him respectfully. She inquired as to what he wanted.

He replied in an almost quivering voice. She could see the fear in his eyes. "Missy, Mr. John is terrible sick and dey sent me to fetch Mr. George. Dey wants him to come right away."

Council's mother asked what was wrong with Uncle John, but the black man did not know. He just repeated what he was told to say. Council's mother told the black man where George could be found and sent him to the fields to find him. When George heard the news, he sent the black man back to Uncle John's to tell the family he was on his way.

Council's father told him to run and get the doctor and meet him at Uncle John's house, which was a few miles down the road from them. Council ran like the wind to go and find the doctor. George took the mule from the field and hooked him to the cart. He stopped at the house and gathered his wife and they left for Uncle John's immediately. By early afternoon the doctor had seen Uncle John and gave the family the distressing news. John was gravely ill and there was nothing anyone could do for him. The family would just have to make him as comfortable as possible and wait for his time to come.

George and his wife gathered Uncle John's things together and placed him gently in the back of the mule and cart, taking him to their home to live out his last days.

When they reached home, some arrangements needed to be made. It was at this time the family turned the front sitting room into a bedroom for Uncle John. This made it possible for John to receive cooling breezes in the spring and summer months and be close to the fire for the cold winter days and nights. It was also the largest room in the house making it much easier for Uncle John to receive visitors such as friends and family. John lingered upon his deathbed for over a year. The following spring the house was opened again as before to air out the odors of being closed all winter, but to also make Uncle John as comfortable as they could. He had all but stopped eating and his lucid moments were few. He lay quietly on his bed never speaking or acknowledging there was anyone in the room other than himself.

Word went out to the family that his time was near and if anyone wished to see him they needed to come as soon as possible. The following Saturday all the family who possibly could made the journey to Council's house to see Uncle John one last time. All the brothers and sisters, cousins, and close neighbors were there to tell John goodbye. The adults sat and stood around the room talking and reminiscing about John and the rest of the family. The children played close by in the hallway leading to the front door. Council's brother left the little troop of children and crept in to take a look at his Uncle. He was quickly dismissed by the adults and told to return to the other children. He made his way across the room and had just gotten to the doorway when he heard a sharp intake of breath coming from Uncle John. All eyes turned to Uncle John's bed.

To the amazement of everyone in the room, a very large black bear came from under the bed and stood mightily on its hind legs and ran from the room, passing everyone including Council's brother. As the bear passed the children in the hallway, they gave chase...only to see it *disappear* before their eyes when it jumped from the front porch.

Council returned to the sick room, wide-eyed and filled with amazement. All of the adults in the room sat unnerved and filled with sorrow at Uncle John's passing. Council asked his father what had happened and where did the bear come from? George looked at his son and told him, "The great bear came from under his bed. That was John's spirit leaving his body. Uncle John is dead."

The years went by and the story is still told, but it is not told with amazement or as an old wive's tale. It is stated as factual and taken seriously. Many would never take this account as factual, but then, the Cherokee and many others will never deny that it can — *and does* — happen.

Chapter Four:

LIGHTS OF MYSTERY

EARLEY STATION

(Hertford County)

Nearly everyone who holds an avid interest in the paranormal have heard the tale of the light at Maco Station, located fourteen miles west of Wilmington in Brunswick County, North Carolina. The light floats and dances in the air, frightening those who see it. Was it the spirit of someone whose life suddenly ended, or a trick of nature? This we may never know; however, the light still appears for us to see. It has been explained in many ways, but no one has ever agreed on the cause or origin of the light. First seen after the train accident that killed Joe Baldwin in the 1800s, it appeared so often that the Atlantic Coastline Railroad was forced to change their signal lights to red and green to end the confusion for the other trains.

Three miles from the Ahoskie city limits in Hertford County was a train crossing named Earley Station. This little-known crossing harbors a secret to those not from the area. There was never an actual station here — no ticket agent or even a stop for the railroad. The closest point to purchase a ticket was Ahoskie. Still it bears the name Earley Station.

The span of track runs from the entrance of the crossing approximately two hundred yards northwest to intersect with another crossing. Since before the 1920s, a single light has been seen along the edge of the tracks, rising and stopping in the center of them. The light then begins to move. It neither floats nor bounces as it makes its way down the track, seemingly toward you.

Many have tried to explain away the light by calling it "swamp gas." However, there is no swampland within miles of this area! Any light coming through the trees from cars creates two lights instead of one and they do not appear as large or of the same color. Both sides of the tracks are heavily wooded, allowing very little, if any, light from the highway to get through.

To be able to see the light, usually a person will park on or near the tracks and wait until the light appears. Gradually, a yellow/orange ball of light will appear along the edge of the tracks and then move to the center of the tracks halfway between the two crossings. The eerie light appears to be the size of a basketball, nearly six to eight feet above the tracks. As you stand still, it will come toward you, moving slowly and steadily up the tracks. The brave souls who dare to walk *toward* the light find themselves within twenty feet of it only to realize the light has begun to back away. The glowing ball of light then disappears at the center of the tracks… *It* gives the appearance of having an intelligence of its own.

Many have been close enough to the light to see from its illumination that there is not a figure attached to it. Through the years, hundreds of people have attempted to analyze what the light could be. They have found no answers. In the 1960s, the Army Corps of Engineers investigated the light for several weeks. They were unable to find a source for it or any reason why it appears when it does. It held none of the properties or values consistent with a natural phenomenon. Their findings were listed as inconclusive.

The summer of 1970 brought together six young men with the determination that they were going to unmask the culprit behind the light. They came together with a plan they felt could not go wrong. Meeting at the crossroads, one of them parked his vehicle at one end of the crossing while the other vehicle parked at the opposite end of the crossing. The moon rose full and high into the night sky, illuminating the area well. The young men waved to each other knowing they could see everything quite clearly. Leaving a man with each vehicle, two from each car walked down the tracks toward each other checking for anyone lying in wait.

There was nothing and no one to be seen, either on the tracks or by the wooded areas. Returning to their cars they stood and waited — and their patience was soon rewarded. Shortly before midnight a small glow appeared by the side of the tracks. They watched intently as it grew in size and made its way up and over the tracks. With an unearthly silence, the light started to move toward the two men standing at the southwest end of the crossing. Nerves on edge, the two men started forward as the men seen clearly at the other end began to walk toward them to meet in the center of the tracks. The light came within ten feet of them and began to move at a faster pace backward away from the two young men. The young men coming from the other end laughed with delight knowing they had the entity trapped.

Near the center of the tracks, the light suddenly wavered as if confused. It could no longer move forward or back. Suddenly the light intensified to almost pure white and disappeared, leaving four young men within forty feet of each other and not knowing what had happened.

It is not known how many people have seen the ghostly light, or how many will see the light in the future. The only thing that is for certain is that the light will appear again and someone will be able to witness an enigma. Reports of lights like the one at Earley Station have been reported in other countries such as India, South Africa, New Zealand, and Great Britain; each with the same characteristics as the light at Earley Station. Still, the question remains: is the light a ghostly spirit or natural phenomena? We may never know for sure and yet we will still endeavor to discover who or what lies beneath the story.

Earley Station does not bring feelings of ghostly images appearing menacingly before you in the dead of night or impending doom like so many other places in this world. With little wonder, you may find yourself ready to go home when the light makes its way into your life... *It's waiting for you.*

BALL OF FIRE

(Hertford County)

In the late 1800s, a small community was formed on the Ahoskie/Cofield Road. This community is called Brantley's Grove. Close to the outer limits of this village is a side road forming a "T" close to Brantley's Grove Baptist Church. This is named "Vann Road" for the many families named Vann that lived down this road. For as long as anyone could remember, the road was never paved until the late 1980s. It was maintained by the state and kept passable even during the harsh conditions of winter. Close to the end of this road are the remains of a one-room school. It is in ruins now, but until the 1970s it was still in good shape and the interior still displayed the old wood stove used for heat. Children from this area rode the bus to school in Ahoskie, three miles from Brantley's Grove.

Three general stores dominated this corner. None were full grocery stores, but you could find the necessities needed to get you by until your next trip into town. Farmers, truck drivers, and anyone else traveling through stopped for refreshments and a snack, or just to catch up on the news. Tales were told of things that had happened in life that as a child one would see as almost ghostly. The story of one lady who had propped her husband on a piano stool and had his portrait taken after his death was scary to a child. Later in life you find such things are not out of the normal for certain time periods.

Brode Denning and his family lived at the corner of the entrance to Vann Road. He was a farmer as his father before him and they had dwelled in the community of Brantley's Grove for many years. His youngest son lived next door and they were always there to help when Brode and his wife became old and were not able to get around as well. Brode's grandson had few friends in the community his age to play with. To be exact, the number of children his age living there could be counted on one hand.

Children in these areas during the 1950s and 60s missed many days of school working on the farms to help the family survive. Their summers were spent fishing, swimming, and working the fields. Many evenings were spent at a friend's house after the work was done. Sometimes they would help each other with the chores so they would have more time to play.

One Saturday afternoon Brode's grandson and his friend were playing a game of catch football near the front porch. Brode and his wife sat on the porch watching them when Brode spoke softly to his wife. Standing from his chair, he told his grandson it was time to go inside and his friend needed to go home. This bothered the grandson's friend, as he had been there many times before and they played well until darkness fell. Some days later they were playing again and the little boy asked Brode's grandson if he had made Mr. Brode angry about anything. The grandson's face became serious. "I need to tell you something, but you don't want to talk about it much. Everybody knows, but they don't say anything."

A little boy's curiosity can run rampant with a statement like that, but soon he was to learn the tale behind it. They sat on the porch in the shade and there he learned the story...

Brode's wife had a brother who passed away many years ago. She had kept his hat and his pocketknife as a memory. As the years rolled by and life puts old memories in the back of your mind she began to think of him more often. One morning she found his hat, which was on the back of the closet shelf, on the floor of the closet. She thought possibly she had moved it and it fell unnoticed by her or Brode. She placed it back on the shelf and went on about her daily routine. The next morning the hat was on the closet floor again. This time no one had touched it. This happened so often she finally decided to leave the hat on the closet floor. The following morning she opened the closet and found the hat back on the closet shelf. She never touched it again.

The little boy asked his friend what that had to do with him going home. Brode's grandson lowered his voice so nobody would hear, but before he could begin Brode came outside and sat on the porch. The grandson looked at him and asked permission to tell his friend about the ball of fire. Brode decided he would tell the story himself, so that there would be no misunderstanding.

"This time of year we don't stay out on the porch until later in the evening. This started when I was just a boy long about your age. Over yonder at the corner of the woods is the old cemetery."

He pointed back toward the edge of the woods about a hundred yards away.

"It was this same time of year, just about dusk and the weather warm like it is now. We were sitting in the yard the first time I saw *it* and I won't forget it. A ball of fire rose up from that graveyard and traveled through the Holly trees. We watched it cross the field about ten feet off the ground. It came right on across the road and then it sped up and hit the side of the house. We thought it was headed for us, but it hit the side of the house by the living room window. After that, it turned away and went back to the cemetery and disappeared. It never left a mark of any kind on the house. That made seeing it happen all the harder to explain. You don't see it every year, but we don't take that chance either. Before you ask, I'll tell you: I been seeing it off and on all my life. The thing has never hurt any of us, but that ain't no sign that it won't. So we leave it alone and hope it will leave us alone."

By the end of the summer, Brode and his family had seen it one more time. They were sitting in the yard beneath one of the huge trees close to the road. Brode's wife saw the ball of fire as it began to rise from the cemetery and warned the others sitting close by. The ball of fire seemed different this time. It was far more intense than it had ever been in previous years. The ball of fire came through the Holly trees at a slow pace, picking up speed as it traveled. It crossed the field, over the dirt road, and bounced as it hit the side of the house.

Without hesitation, it moved straight across the road to the back porch of the Percy Jenkins house, completely missing the store sitting next to the house. Here the ball of fire hit the porch and moved directly back toward the cemetery. All watched while the ball of fire made its way to the trees and disappeared. The family was to find out later the ball of fire actually left ashes on the back porch of the Jenkins house without burning anything! Within a year of this hap-

From the corner of the field behind the house and horse pasture is the old cemetery where the ball of fire originated. It slowly rose and then crossed the field and road to bounce off the home of Brent Dilday.

Brent Dilday points to the spot where a ball of fire from the cemetery across the road bounced off the side of the house.

pening, Mr. Percy Jenkins passed away. Coincidence? As of this date, no one has reported ever seeing the ball of fire again.

Since other incidents aside from the hat being moved in the closet had occurred in the house as well, Brode's family naturally associated the ball of fire with the uncle. There are some, however, who call this phenomenon Foxfire, or a Jack-o'-lantern, or even swamp gas. If this was the case, how can its last movements be so readily dismissed and called "natural?" Brode's family — and other people who have witnessed the ball of fire through the years — are quick to tell you it was anything but natural.

Chapter Five:

LIVING WITH GHOSTS

THE WHITE HOUSE

(Hertford County)

There is only one Ahoskie. The name and the town are very unique in its history and its residents. It is a small town with only 4,523 residents according to the 2000 census. It was once the hub of Hertford County and the surrounding area with manufacturing and farming even before the Civil War. The original name of the town was Ahotsky, given to the residents by the Wyanoke Indians. It has been the home of many great men and celebrities including Major Joe Howard of the United States Air Force Thunderbirds flying team.

Europeans had a slight problem with the name Ahotsky because of its pronunciation, so it was eventually changed to Ahoskie. In the 1950s and 1960s, you could still find the railroad station in the center of town doing business as usual with the freight trains coming through. On Main Street, you could stop by the local drug stores and sit down for an ice-cold milk shake or soda to ease the heat of the day. The aroma of Harrell's Bakery made one's mouth water for the finest cakes, pies, and doughnuts anywhere to be found. Should a repair be needed, you could go to the blacksmith shop nearby that was owned by a veteran of the Civil War. It was a town in which everybody knew your name. They all cared for each other and tried to lead you in the right direction.

During this time, it was not hard to find that the town was steeped in Native American history. Even the high school teams were named

The white house is now over one hundred years old and in need of repair. The paranormal happenings in this home were many and commonplace.

as such with the mascot being an Indian Chief. A favorite stop for students after school was the local bus station. It was here they found hamburgers and hot dogs that had a taste all its own and were reasonably priced. A visit to the Tomahawk Restaurant was in order for a full meal. On Friday nights and Saturday afternoons, a trip downtown would find you listening to young people standing on the street corner by the movie theater singing songs in small groups. All of these things barely scrape the surface of a good life for the residents of this town.

Mike grew up in this town. He attended and graduated from the local schools. Several times during his life, he lived with his grandparents in a large, two-story house situated on a section of the Old Stagecoach Road. Everybody knew the house as the "White House." It had an upstairs that consisted of two bedrooms and a long hallway that led to the stairs. Upstairs there was only one closet and it was just deep and wide enough to hang a suit or coat flat against the wall. The windows throughout the house were of an old style and very large with three bays each looking out over the front porch and the street. The main portion of the house was the downstairs and had a bedroom to the right of the main hall and a closet beneath the stairway. To your left, upon entering the house, you would find a formal sitting room that was used for a bedroom. Following through the door, there was a small sitting room where guests were entertained and the next room was the kitchen. A narrow back porch ran half the length of the kitchen and sitting room combined due to the addition of a more modern and convenient bathroom.

Many times people will ride down a street in these small towns and their attention is drawn to a particular house on that block. It is not a fancy house, nor are there any particular features that stand out. It is usually very plain or you just like the shade of the trees in the yard. At the same time, you are intrigued and wish to stay in this house, though something deep inside tells you it would not be wise. This is the sort of house where Mike spent a large amount of his life.

We're Not Alone...

Growing up he became accustomed to strange things about the house that were *not* happening in the homes of his friends. As a child, he first began to notice things were out of place. You could not really pinpoint what they were, so they were just called "things." Sitting in the shade in the backyard with his family, many times he would look toward the window in the hallway upstairs. It gave him a very pronounced feeling of someone standing there watching him. He would then force himself to turn away just to take one more look to be sure. The feeling had passed as quickly as it had come. Inside the big house, he began to notice something very odd. Light always filters deep into the next room if the ceiling lights are on. He knew this to be true because a ceiling light was always far brighter than a lamp and yet light from one room would only travel a maximum of twelve inches into the next room and the rest of that room would be pitch black. You had an odd sensation when entering that room, but it was never scary.

His grandmother and grandfather never used the front door after darkness fell. If you were sleeping upstairs, they would unlock their doors and let you out into the hall only to hear the locks being bolted behind you. The bedroom door leading to the downstairs hall had five different locks including a chain. Then for added security a chair was placed beneath the door handle to prevent the door from opening. The door leading to the bathroom from the sitting room had three locks and the door in the kitchen leading to the porch had four locks including a sliding bolt. All of these locks were put to use by the end of the evening. Being young and curious, Mike asked his grandparents why they had so many locks. He did not feel they had anything to be afraid of. The answer he received was not what he expected. His grandfather sat in silence, but his grandmother pulled him closer, her voice becoming very serious and unusually calm. She told him never to unlock the hallway doors after dark for anything and to cut the light on before entering the hallway after dark. She said there were things that most people did not know about and you wanted to stay away from them. Grandfather did not disagree; he just looked the other way.

Mike already knew that when you were upstairs, you were *not* alone. You could feel it, sense it…like you were wearing an extra coat. He grew up with these feelings and became accustomed to them and his fear abated. Strange sights or sounds no longer affected him as they did others. To this day, his sisters refuse to enter the old house.

The years rolled by and soon Mike wanted to fix his room upstairs in a manner that suited him. He cleaned it well and painted the walls and trim as well as the floor and rearranged the furniture. He had tried the bedroom downstairs across the hall without success. When the bed was in the corner of the room, he would have nightmares so horrific, he became physically ill. Strangely he could never remember the dream. The bedroom across the hall and the upstairs always gave him a sensation of not belonging to the rest of the house. When the bed was turned to line against the wall all was well, but the room became extremely cold. It was time to relocate his sleeping quarters, which he did. This was when he redecorated the bedroom upstairs. He was happy and slept well for many months without an occurrence.

However, no good thing lasts forever. He lay in bed sleeping when around 1 o'clock in the morning he awoke without reason. He was fully awake and wondering why he didn't want to close his eyes. Sitting straight up in bed, he stared at the closed bedroom door as if expecting someone. Without warning, he heard the sound of a hurricane-like wind come down the hallway upstairs and stop at the head of the stairs. A sound as loud as a wrecking ball being rolled down the stairs reverberated throughout the house. At the bottom of the stairs, he heard the sound of heavy boots walk from the bottom of the stairs around to the closet beneath the steps. When the footsteps ended, the silence was almost deafening. He could not believe what he had heard, but he was still not frightened. The following morning, he asked about the sounds he had heard during the night. Everyone at the breakfast table acted as though it was a normal thing to hear. They had heard the sound several times over the years they had lived there, but the sound was never heard but once downstairs.

These are the kinds of things you do not discuss with your friends and so Mike kept them to himself. His friends were never asked to spend the night as long as he lived at his grandparent's home. Months later his mother was hanging out laundry to dry in the sun. As she stood hanging the clothes, she heard a woman call her name.

She looked around, but there was no one in sight and she knew the grandparents were out of state visiting their daughter. She dismissed the occurrence as having her mind on too many things. When she returned to the old house, she put down her laundry basket and entered the back door. To her surprise, she heard someone walking upstairs. She knew the children were all at school and her husband was working. She was supposed to be the only person in the house. Quickly she went to the stairs and called out. Nobody answered. Gathering her courage, she ascended the stairs and walked into the room where the sounds were coming from — there was no one there and no place to hide. These sounds were heard often, but that did not make it any less unnerving when you went to check on a possible unwanted visitor.

Checking in...

In 1975, Mike's grandmother passed away, leaving his grandfather alone after a very long marriage. He stayed with his grandfather in the room he had made for himself upstairs and kept his grandfather company. His parents also came to stay with him and occupied the downstairs bedroom across the hall. When Mike first came home from the Marines, his first night back in the old house, he slept on a single bed by the upstairs window until his room was ready again. To his amazement, the bed rocked him to sleep on several nights. He then regained his old bedroom and changed it back to the way it was when he was younger. A few months after his grandmother had passed away, he was laying in

The kitchen is located here at the back of the house. Late one night, it was bathed in a mysterious blue light. There was no moon out and the sky was nearly pitch black. This was within a year of the former resident's death.

bed thinking of what he may want to do with his life. He was looking toward the closed door of the bedroom when he saw the door open about ten inches. He could also see that the *real* door was still closed. The ghostly door stood open as he witnessed seeing the head of his grandmother peer around the edge of the door, nod her head at him, and close the unearthly door securely shut. The opening door never made a sound. He sat unnerved yet very unsettled. She had never checked on him at bedtime even when she was alive! He told his parents what he had seen and agreed not to say anything to his grandfather.

During the winter months, his grandfather would go to visit with his daughter in Virginia. Mike's mother would go check on the house and make sure everything was clean while Mike was staying there. While Mike was at work, she came in one afternoon. When she entered the sitting room, she heard the noise of someone moving about upstairs. She made her way into the hallway and reached for a stick inside the hallway closet. She neared the bottom of the stairs and called out. No one answered. She called out again and demanded an answer or she was more than willing to hurt whoever was in the house. Still receiving no answer, she climbed the stairs and entered the bedroom. To her dismay, she saw the rug that was under the grandmother's rocking chair was pulled back and partially under the bed. The rocking chair itself was just beginning to stop rocking. This chair did not rock easily even with someone in it. The legs had been wired to each other just to keep it from falling apart. She put the rug back into place, setting the old rocker back on top of it, and left the room. She never returned again alone. When she did return, the rocking chair was once more on bare floor and the rug pulled back. Mike's grandmother used this old rocking chair until it was no longer safe to sit in.

Spring arrived once more and the joys of sitting in the shade and talking were back. Spring turns to summer and you find yourself at the end of a long day sitting and talking with the old folks. Mike arrived home from work and was enjoying the time he was spending with his grandfather. There were times they would talk and barely say anything, but a full conversation was held. Some may find this a hard thing to accomplish, but when you know someone really well you don't have to say much. Mike's grandfather sat in his wheelchair and chuckled lightly at a small joke he had told. The old man was not prone to lengthy conversation, but when he spoke you listened. He knew his time was not far off and age had taken its toll on him. He was still very strong and determined with a quick mind. He missed his wife, but he did not dwell on her being gone from his life.

During this conversation, the grandmother had not been mentioned in their conversation. A silence fell between them as it often did, but Mike understood and said nothing, just sitting quietly. The back door to the old house stood open so the heat of the day could escape. As if on queue, both Mike and his grandfather looked toward the back door. There they saw the grandmother dressed in her sun-bonnet and old housedress appearing halfway in the doorway. She looked at them and nodded and began to slowly pull back out of sight. Mike's grandfather turned and hung his head saying nothing. To Mike it was more than obvious his grandfather had witnessed the same thing he had. They never discussed seeing her, but in their own way they made it plain to each other that neither was wrong in what they saw. Two years later Mike's grandfather died at the home of his daughter in Virginia. Men of his caliber are never forgotten.

Paranormal activity in this house was higher than most cases that are reported. Mike and his family can tell many more stories that are uncanny about this old Southern home. Residents who have lived in the house since the passing of the old man never stated they experienced anything, and yet not one of these families have stayed in the house for very long.

A RAP UPON MY DOOR

(Chowan County)

It was a peaceful place, one where a man and a woman could sit outside on the deck and enjoy the sunshine while feeling a soothing breeze brush across their skin. The gentle lapping of the small waves as they rolled upon the shore lulled the senses into a mild euphoria. Along the shores of the Chowan River, near the town of Edenton, rests two small mobile homes. They were originally intended for vacation spots, but as the owners grew, so did their taste for bigger and better things. The vacation spot was then rented out to people who wanted the shore life, but could not afford the vacation homes of the affluent and their lifestyles.

Over the centuries, famous pirates sailed these waters and plotted ways to barter and trade their stolen goods, as well as provide a safe haven for themselves and their families. Blackbeard being the most infamous of the lot, his residence was only a few miles from this spot.

Scott and Brenda sought out such a place where they could live and enjoy their life on the meager salaries they received from their labors. It was here they could go fishing whenever they were ready and entertain family and friends. Scott worked for the owner of this mobile home and the owner was very fond of him. He worked hard and the owner treated him like a second son. Within a few months, the mobile home became vacant and the owner offered it for rent to Scott and Brenda at a very low price. He told Scott he felt he didn't have to worry about the home being abused with Scott and Brenda living there and that they could stay as long as they wished.

The resident next door was an affable person and the two of them got along well. They fished together, hunted together, and a cook out was just not complete without his new friend. The first year went very well and the couple was happier than they could possibly imagine. They both had gotten raises in salary and their lifestyle was moving up.

Late one evening, while Scott and Brenda had friends over, all the men sat down by the shoreline drinking beer and telling stories. The tales slowly made their way around to some of the old tales of pirates and ghosts. Scott's father had gotten more than a little drunk and asked Scott's neighbor for a good ghost tale. Scott's neighbor's face took on a serious look and he took a long swallow of beer before he replied, "Scott can give you some better stories than I can. That place he lives in is loaded with ghosts or something, but it ain't natural either way you go."

Scott had no idea what to say. He had not seen or heard anything out of the ordinary since he and Brenda had moved in. The jibes went around the small group of men and the subject of Scott's home was dismissed. The following morning Scott saw his neighbor and they sat to talk while nursing the mother of all hangovers. Scott tried to inquire as to what his neighbor was talking about the night before when the talk turned to ghosts. The neighbor laughed good-naturedly and told Scott he was just joking a little. The look on the man's face did little to convince Scott he was telling the truth.

Something's There...

The following September brought a celebration for the happy couple. It was their fourth wedding anniversary and they made plans to go into Edenton and have dinner at a local seafood restaurant. Scott had gotten dressed and sat in the living room waiting for his wife to finish doing her hair and looking her best for their evening out together. Suddenly, Brenda cried out. It was a cry you would hear that bordered fear and pain combined. Scott rushed to the bathroom and burst through the door. He found his wife leaning against the wall crying. She said she was slipping into her new dress when "something" slapped her very hard on her hip. Raising her dress Scott saw an entire handprint on her thigh that was already turning black and blue with bruising. He could understand if she fell and hit the shower door or maybe even the edge of the sink, but neither of these would leave a solid handprint! She was frightened, but they were both so bewildered as to what had just happened. Complete understanding was just not feasible at the moment. They hurried out of the house and left for their dinner engagement. They could not enjoy themselves as they might have, but they were not about to let the incident ruin their evening. After much celebration, the incident was all but forgotten for the night.

The next day, at 7 o'clock in the morning, a rap came upon the back door of the mobile home. Scott rose from bed, slid on his trousers, and opened the door. There was no one to be seen. Scott looked around — there was only his car in the driveway. He then thought maybe his neighbor had come to visit and then changed his mind when the door was not answered quickly. This began to happen every morning without fail. It mattered not how long he took to get to the door. At times the rap would continue just as long as he stayed in bed and stopped immediately as soon as his feet hit the floor. If Scott was already awake and rambling about the house, the rap still came on the back door, but never when he was close to it. The rapping was always at 7 o'clock in the morning. After some months of this, Scott confided in his neighbor that he thought he had a ghost in his house. He told him of the rapping that occurred every morning and about Brenda being slapped hard enough to leave bruising. His neighbor listened quietly and when he had finished he asked Scott if that was all that had happened. Scott stated that one morning every faucet in the house came on at the same time, but that was only the one time.

Scott's neighbor said nothing at first and then slowly began to tell Scott his story. He said he had moved into the other trailer about a year or so before Scott and Brenda came to live there. After about a month, every morning the kitchen cabinet doors would be open. He would shut them and go about his business and nothing more would happen. There were times he would wake in the middle of the night or early morning only to hear his shower or the kitchen faucets running wide open. Sometimes the toilet flushed with him standing next to it while shaving. He had not touched any of these things — they operated on their own accord. He never felt that he was alone in the trailer and had seen things like shadows cross the room several times. Whenever he saw them, he usually got dressed and went outside for awhile. The only time he had ever been scared was the morning he awoke from a solid sleep to hear a woman singing in his closet.

Scott asked him why he had not moved. His answer was mildly surprising. He said he started to move several times and each time he had feelings of unrepressed sadness and could not bring himself to finish the move.

The fall of that year brought about the end of the hurricane season. A fifty-foot tall pine

Around the point from this small bay is the former home for two families that rented mobile homes — they were the scene of a haunting like none other. The land was eventually sold and a private residence now occupies the space.

tree grew close to the end of Scott and Brenda's home. During the course of the night the pine tree was uprooted in a hard wind and fell to the ground. It completely missed their bedroom by inches. The huge pine tree or the sound of a mighty wind was never heard as the tree slammed to the ground behind where they slept.

Were their lives protected by the ghosts of this house? It is a question we will never know. A human life can be a fleeting thing, but the spirit of man goes on forever.

ROCKY HOCK

(Chowan County)

Who's Unlocking the Door?

George Washington Smith was the son of an English immigrant who came to the United States in the early 1800s. George and his wife, Viola Byrd, with their children, made their home in a beautiful two-story colonial style house on Rocky Hock Landing Road, which leads directly to the Chowan River, a mere mile away. This road is located on Highway 32, a few miles from Edenton, which was once the provincial capital of North Carolina. A point of interest for this area lies in the fact that Edenton was heavily involved with assisting members of the Boston Tea Party. This small feat in history is known as the Edenton Tea Party. The ladies boycotted any use or purchasing of tea that was taxed by England through the East India Tea Company.

George made his living as a commercial fisherman and farmer. Those who knew him considered him and his wife a handsome and sensible couple with good standing among the community. George labored hard to provide for his family and spent his evening hours attending his family and enjoying life with them. He offered all the protection for his young children a man can possibly render.

From the first day George and Viola moved into the Colonial house they discovered something very strange. Each evening before going to bed George or Viola would lock the double doors that served as the entrance to the house. Each morning they would find the doors unlocked and sometimes open. George did everything possible to secure the doors of the home. One morning he examined the doors carefully and could find nothing wrong with the locks. Being a man of sensibility, he came to the conclusion that it may be something he was not capable of detecting or repairing. He went to Edenton and bought fine new locks for the doors and installed them. After testing them, he found the doors were secure and he was happy. The following morning he came downstairs and discovered the doors were again unlocked. George knew he had closed the top bolt for the opposite door and locked with his key, the new locks; still they were found unlocked with no sign of an intruder.

Neither he nor his family ever found anything missing nor was there ever any sign of an intruder. It did not matter how late they stayed awake waiting to see the doors unlock themselves; at some point they would again be found silently unlocked and they never saw a single thing to cause this phenomenon. George and Viola stayed in this home for sixteen years before relocating to Gates County, North Carolina, but the mystery of the unlocked doors was never solved. The Smith family and its descendants have never ventured far from the shores of the Chowan River and a few who did venture out always returned.

In this beautiful farm country, history has made its mark upon not only the United States, but also the world as we know it, from the Revolutionary War to what Chowan County is today. For those who believe in life after death, they fully believe that ghosts exists in a land such as this. It has seen the good as well as the bad in life and witnesses say they have seen the unknown in their every day lives.

Who's Coming to Dinner?

Mary Sue purchased a small plot of land bordering Rocky Hock and built a small clapboard house. The home was small by some standards, but for her it was perfect. She was a widow. Her husband had recently died after a long and very expensive illness. Her children all came together and had the house built for her, so she would be close to them. It was a blessing to have her nearby so they could watch over her.

Mary Sue smiled broadly the first time she entered the house. It was hard for her to conceive that the house was hers and she did not owe a penny for it. Mary Sue knew she was blessed to have children as caring as hers seemed to be. Two of her sons had built most of the house and installed every convenience they felt she might need to keep her comfortable in her later years.

The day the children moved her into the new house Mary's daughter remarked to her brothers about the odd look in her mother's eyes when she went in. Her oldest son sidled up to Mary

Sue and wrapped his arms around her gently, "Is there anything else you need to make you happy, Mother?" he asked softly. Her reply brought a look of mild dismay to his face. "I don't know of another thing I need in this world. I have all of you and your father to keep me company."

Her son did not want to remind her that her husband and their father was deceased, so he just smiled and told her he would go and leave her to settle in at her own pace. He never told the others about his mother's words.

The children all gathered at their Mother's house the following Thanksgiving for dinner. They had begun to notice a change had come over her. She began to set the table for them to eat their dinner and placed an extra plate at the head of the table. Her daughter immediately asked if they were having an extra guest for the holiday. The daughter thought there might be an uncle or cousin coming to surprise them. Her mother smiled sweetly and told her that was her father's plate and to make sure he had his glass of water as he didn't like tea. Her daughter knew she was getting old and let the incident pass. She did, however, let her brothers know what was happening.

From that day forward they all began to watch her closely and visit every day without fail. Mary Sue set a plate for her deceased husband every day and filled the plate as if he were going to eat. One evening her oldest son stayed for dinner and watched as his mother filled the plate and then sat down for her meal. He asked her about the plate at the head of the table. Mary Sue was quick to reply that his father would be there any minute and she wanted his supper to be on time. Her son sat and listened as she talked and then he heard footsteps in the short hallway and the closing of the front door. He rose from his chair to see who was coming into the house. His mother reached out, holding his arm lightly, and told him to "sit still... *it's* only your father." Her son could hardly believe his ears. She talked to the empty chair just as if his father was actually sitting there. None of the food disappeared from the plate, but the sound of the chair creaking was almost more than he could take. When the meal was over, he heard the footsteps descend down the hall and the opening and closing of the front door. His mother smiled sweetly as she picked up the dinner plate that had been set out for her husband. She sighed lightly, "Your father's appetite is not what it was, but he was really happy to see you."

With these words still ringing in his ears, he excused himself and went home. The following day her son visited the local minister to ask him how to handle what he had seen and heard. The Pastor volunteered to visit her and see for himself the next day. After the pastor had paid his visit, he contacted Mary Sue's family and met with them at the church. He could not explain what he had seen and heard and still she was doing no harm to herself or anyone else. He told them there are many things on this earth that only God can account for. The conclusion: let her be happy as long as she can.

Through the years the children came every day, sometimes twice a day, to visit Mary Sue and things never changed. They did not discuss their father with her and the table was always set with one more plate until she died peacefully in her sleep on a warm September night. The family had eventually agreed that there was someone in their mother's life that they were unable to see or be in contact with. The answers to all their questions and troubles always seemed to be waiting for them when they came to Mary Sue's for dinner. In her words, "Your father said not to worry...it will work itself out."

You may say this was an answer of generalities... The unexplainable happened to be the specific answers and advice received.

THE GHOST OF WILLIE

(Currituck County)

Nancy Peterson and her family had lived in a house located near the small fishing village of Coinjock for several years. She had always thought how lucky she was to have a loving family and everything peaceful. Then came her winter of discontent. Her husband left them for someone else and they never heard from him again. This left her alone with two children and more bills than she knew about before he deserted them.

The house was average in appearance and the rent was reasonable, but on her salary she needed help. Her mother was a widow of many years and moved in with them; this enabled them to help each other out with living expenses. Nancy gave the main bedroom to her mother and began sleeping in one of the back bedrooms close to the children. After her husband had left them, she no longer desired to sleep in the same bedroom.

Shortly after her mother came to live with them, the haunting began. Her mother came into the kitchen to help Nancy fix breakfast one morning and her mood was less than amiable. Nancy asked her what was wrong. Her mother quickly told her that she needed to make less noise when she was getting clothes out of her closet after she had gone to bed. Nancy asked her what she was talking about. She assured her mother she had not gone into the bedroom the night before. Nancy's mother turned on her very angry. "You woke me up when you came in the room and it sounded as though you were going to tear the closet apart for whatever you were looking for."

Nancy once again denied being in the room and the subject was forgotten when the children came into the kitchen. The incident plagued Nancy's thoughts for the rest of the day. Two nights later Nancy's mother was awakened again by someone coming into the room and rambling through the closet. She could not contain her anger and reached for the lamp beside the bed. Switching it on, the light flooded the bedroom and to her dismay there was no one in the room with her. She lay awake for the rest of the night, unable to sleep, wondering what had happened. She did not feel as though she was dreaming and still she was not sure.

When the sun rose into a beautiful Carolina sky, she jumped from her bed and found her daughter busy fixing breakfast. She told her what had happened and apologized for thinking it had been her. Nancy's mother was quick to tell her that while she did not believe in ghosts...*something* was in the house besides the family!

Nancy laughed lightly and told her mother she may have just been dreaming and it just seemed real. The rest of the day passed pleasantly and the incident was placed to the back of their minds. That evening they cooked their food on the grill and then went inside to watch a movie. Nancy's mother put the kids to bed and they both settled in on the sofa for a quiet evening. When the commercial came on, Nancy left the sofa to get them something to drink. She was already about five feet passed the television when it cut itself off. Nancy's mother sneered playfully. "You know I might have wanted to see that ad on TV if it's not too much trouble." Nancy laughed, "Don't turn it off if you want to watch it."

They both watched as the television *turned itself on* and changed channels. Neither Nancy or her mother were near the TV when it changed channels, nor was the remote close to either of them. This began to happen at the most inconvenient of times. They eventually bought a new TV, thinking the one they had was defective. Once, while she was walking to the front door to leave, it came on by itself and flipped through the channels. Nancy turned it off and left the house. When she returned, it was back on and the volume was turned up very loud. There was not another house within a mile, so they ruled out someone on the same wavelength with a remote control. The same incidents started occurring with the new TV.

Nancy finally had enough. She screamed out to nothing while looking about the room. "Okay ghost, if you got a name tell me now and quit playing with us!" A voice came to her from nowhere and everywhere at the same time, "Willie."

She was stunned, but she started talking to Willie each time something happened. Nancy's three-year-old son was playing quietly in the kitchen as she washed the morning dishes. She turned just in time to see a toy truck roll from the refrigerator over to where the child sat on the floor. Nancy gathered her nerve and began to talk to the ghost in her home.

Nancy and her mother asked nicely for Willie to stop moving the children's toys when they were playing with them. Obediently the movements stopped in the children's room as well as the other rooms in the house. Kitchen utensils would be moved or disappear altogether, but were always returned when asked. Jewelry appeared on two occasions on the kitchen table that belonged neither to Nancy or her mother. They disappeared days later not to be found.

Nancy found all of this to be very wearing on their nerves. They asked around the community and found there was nobody known

The ghost of Willie is an enigma for all. No one ever lived in the house by the name of Willie and still he made his presence known to its occupants. In the end, he followed this family to a new home.

as Willie as far as they could remember. The former tenant in the house worked in Elizabeth City for a construction company and moved when he was transferred to a town in the north.

The ghostly happenings continued for almost a year and then stopped as suddenly as they began.

The house was never the same after Willie left, but Nancy and her mother did not miss the antics of the ghost. Years later Nancy remarried after her mother died and moved to a newer home. A few short weeks after they moved in, the TV turned on by itself. Nancy

smiled and said, "Long time no see Willie. How ya been?" Her new husband, who was sitting beside her, inquired, "Who is Willie?" Her only answer to the question was a big smile and a gentle hug.

NO PLACE TO CALL HOME

(Hertford County)

The streets of Ahoskie, North Carolina, are often lined with old and very large shade trees. A leisurely walk down these streets can be quite refreshing on a warm summer day. One of the prettiest streets there is Church Street, with many of its houses dating back into the 1920s. You will find large, two-story homes with ten-foot high ceilings and the windows your grandparents spoke of. They were built to cycle as much air as possible because they were built before the use of home air-conditioning.

There is a lot of family history within the walls of these old homes. Yet one stands out among the rest for its contribution to the community. The older populace of Ahoskie can tell you this was no ordinary house. It was once the funeral parlor for Lumstead Funeral Home. Today it is in the process of being remodeled for private occupancy.

The house has large shade trees and gives the appearance of being the same as any other place one would desire to live. The east end of the house bears a sun room for those quiet evenings at home or an afternoon nap in the shade. It has eight to ten rooms depending on what you would like to use them for. At the rear of the house is a large kitchen with good lighting. These are just a few of its qualities that would draw someone to want to stay within these walls.

Mr. Lumstead started the business here shortly after World War I. He was an extraordinary man with a fine sense of humor. Those who knew him reported Mr. Lumstead as being tall and thin, but strong physically as well as morally. During his time as a soldier in the United States Army, he was seriously wounded in combat by an artillery shell exploding near him. From his rib cage all the way across his stomach, he laid open with his intestines in danger of falling from his body. He knew he would die if he did not get help soon, but he also knew there was no one able to help him in his position. With a bravery few men could ever muster, Mr. Lumstead ripped up his shirt and sewed himself together using the shirt for sutures. He then traveled across the battlefield until he found someone to tend him medically.

Mr. Lumstead lived for a very long time after the war was over and he lived his life to the fullest. He opened his business caring for the concerns of the community. There was always a great respect for those who had lost loved ones. Everyone knew Mr. Lumstead genuinely cared about their losses.

No one can live forever and there came the time when Mr. Lumstead died. He was laid to rest in Ahoskie Cemetery, where he still remains a respected man for those who knew him. His funeral parlor became a rental property in later years and was vacant often. You never heard anything bad about the house and yet no one stayed for long.

Still Tending to Business?

In the 1960s, Buddy and his wife wanted to build themselves a new house. The house they wanted to build was of custom design for the times and it would be many months before it would be completed. Buddy knew the owner of Mr. Lumstead's house and contacted him about

Formerly the Lumstead Funeral Home, this building is now a private residence undergoing renovation. The building was a rental property for several years; the tenants reported hearing unusual noises coming from all over the house.

renting the property until his new home was completed. The deal was struck, and soon Buddy and his wife were moving into the former funeral home.

The couple settled in and were surprised at how roomy and comfortable the house seemed to be. Buddy often wondered why the owners had so much trouble keeping tenants. Months went by and sometimes they would hear something out of the ordinary, but they paid no attention to the strange sounds.

One afternoon, shortly after lunch, Buddy's wife was feeling very tired. She went into the living room and lay down on their new sofa to sleep for awhile. She felt she would nap for an hour or so and then get back to cleaning the house before Buddy got home from work.

She drifted off into a sound peaceful sleep, but was awakened by the sound of footsteps walking across the bare wooden floors of the

next room. Thinking her husband had come home early, she left the sofa and went into the kitchen to start supper for the night. Changing her mind, she went to the room where she had heard the footsteps with the intention of asking her husband why he was home so early. To her dismay, she found no one there. She walked into each room of the house and realized she was alone. Knowing she had been sleeping, she was quick to think she had been dreaming when she heard the sounds. This was a little confusing to her. The footsteps were heard with great clarity. She could have sworn they were the footsteps of a man walking into the other room.

Buddy came home that night after a long day and listened to his wife's story as he ate his supper. He laughed and told her she had to have been dreaming and didn't realize it. She denied this, swearing she was fully awake at the time. For a time, the story was dismissed, as other topics became of more importance.

Buddy stood before the mirror shaving while getting ready for another day at work. From behind him, through the closed bathroom door, he heard someone walk by. Not giving this any thought, he assumed his wife had gotten out of bed and was going to the kitchen for coffee. When he had finished shaving, he cleaned his face and walked out of the bathroom... His wife was still in bed fast asleep!

Buddy's wife came from the grocery store and placed her purchases on the kitchen table. She made herself busy for the next hour putting things away and starting to prepare the evening meal. It was a pleasant day outside and she wanted to get some flowers planted in the yard before it became too dark to see. As she turned to pick up her things for planting, she started hearing someone talking. She stopped and listened. The words were indistinct, but the voices seemed clear. She started through the house, but the voices seemed to always stay ahead of her. When she was downstairs, the voices were upstairs. Traveling up the stairwell, she found herself checking each room, finding them completely void of any life other than her own. It was then she noticed that the voices were coming from downstairs. Still there was never a soul to be found and the voices finally trailed off into nothing.

The same incident happened one evening while Buddy sat

watching television. He turned the sound all the way down and could hear someone talking, and yet there was no one in the house but him.

The voices and the sounds of footsteps continued now and again for the rest of their time within the walls of this house. They never felt uneasy nor were they ever frightened. It was just a curiosity.

Chapter Six:

A LARK OF NATURE?

MONEY IN A JAR

(Bertie County)

Charley Wynn and his wife of twenty years, Bess, struggled hard to make ends meet. The Great Depression was in full swing and people did what they could to keep food on the table. Charley owned a small farm in a rural community of Eastern North Carolina called Colerain. The farm held rich land, ripe for planting. The problem being, there was no money for seed and almost no market to sell the crops. Though the farm passed down through the generations to the eldest son, this was the first year it ever lay idle to the hands that toiled in the fields.

Charley and his wife were fine, hard-working people in the community and attended the local church on a regular basis. They tended a small garden in the back of the house, chopped wood, repaired wagons, and also did some work for the WPA just to stay even, if not a touch ahead. These things helped greatly, but still money was scarce.

In the evenings, the local farmers usually met at a nearby general store to visit and try to find out the latest news they possibly had not heard. It was pleasant to sit on the benches and share old stories with his friends. It gave them all an opportunity to forget their problems for just awhile and feel life was normal again.

Winter came early that year and the rain fell upon the little community in torrents. Thunderstorms dominated the skies above them, making life more difficult than it already was. One dark rainy evening, Charley returned early from his visit to the general store. He had hurried home to make certain his wife was okay. They sat in the parlor, talking late into the night and smiling about the good things to come.

Bess arose from her chair by the fire and went into the kitchen for a drink of water. She stood for a brief moment at the kitchen window, staring out into the storm. The thunder rolled heavily in the distance while a sudden flash of lightning illuminated the house and the fields around them. Through the window, she saw a man with a shovel standing close to the huge ancient Oak by the edge of the woods. When the lightning flashed once more, she could see him digging diligently by the tree through the pouring rain.

She called to her husband and asked him to look at the stranger. When the lightning lit up the skies around them once more, there was no one to be seen. Charley laughed lightly and said she was imagining things. Bess laughed with him, but never changed her mind about what she had witnessed.

Several nights later, the stranger appeared once again and this time it was Charley, not Bess, who saw him. He stood by the window and watched for several minutes as the stranger dug at the soil with a passion. At the next flash of lightning, the stranger disappeared as suddenly as he had appeared before Charley's disbelieving eyes.

Charley made his way to the general store for his nightly visit with the guys the following evening. After a great deal of consideration, he decided to share his story with his friends. He was not ridiculed as he thought he would be. Charley's friends and neighbors sat quietly listening to his story. When he had finished, each man gave his opinion.

Charley's friend, Richard Little, stared at Charley for an instant and coughed. Everyone standing had turned their attention toward him. "Charley, if the old folks are right, you need to dig where you saw that fella at. You never know what you might find. I heard folks tell of finding money and jewelry and lord knows what digging behind a ghost."

Charley smiled at his friend. "With my luck, the only thing I would find is a deeper hole."

The men laughed uneasily. They were superstitious and a ghost was not to be taken lightly. Charley bid his friends good night and hurried home. He slept fitfully through the night, worried about the welfare of his wife and family. The light of morning did not bear good news for him. He stood by the woodpile smoking his pipe and watched as the postman drove into the yard. He signed for a letter from the Bertie County Tax Department and watched the postman as he drove away down the lane back to the highway.

Tearing open the envelope, he read the worst news he could ever have imagined. The letter stated he had until the following Friday to pay forty-seven dollars in property taxes or they would auction his farm. Charley and Bess would be homeless!

With a heavy heart, Charley sat down with Bess and read her the letter. His heart sank as he watched her weeping, and there was nothing he could do to comfort her. Forty-seven dollars could very well have been forty-seven million. He had nothing left to sell and no way to produce the money to save his farm.

He returned to the general store that evening with his heart in his hands. Several more of his friends had received the same letter. The men thought of everything conceivable to raise enough money to keep from losing their homes, and yet they knew it would never be enough to save them all.

Charley walked home with his head low and listened to the thunder rolling in the distance. He stepped onto the porch and hugged his wife gently as he shook his head. She knew in her heart that he had not been able to get the money needed so badly.

On Thursday night, the rain fell heavily, filling the yard and fields with much unwanted water. The ditches by the roadside swelled and spilled into the road, flooding everything. Charley and Bess sat in the kitchen wondering where they would go and talked of the heartbreak of losing their home. Blinding light filled the sky as the lightning flashed. Bess went to the sink and filled a glass of water for herself and Charley. She hung her head and filled the glass slowly and the tears began to come.

A horrific clap of thunder rattled the very eves of the house as the lightning flashed. It was then that she saw the figure by the old Oak tree with his shovel. Bess turned to her husband and, smiling, said, "Your ghost is back. I guess he is the only one that will tend these fields after tomorrow. If you do not mind, I think I will go to bed. A prayer or two might not hurt either of us."

Charley kissed her good night and watched her walk away. Turning to the kitchen window, he saw the figure again as the skies above flashed lightning and the thunder rolled. Charley grabbed his hat and coat from the hook by the door, and hurried out into the storm. The sound of his friend's voice rang in his ears:

"YOU NEVER KNOW WHAT YOU MIGHT FIND!"

He grabbed his pick and shovel as he raced past the barn. The mud, deep around his ankles, threatened to throw him down. Twice he fell into the mud and twice he regained his footing. Lightning filled the sky and struck the ancient Oak, all but destroying it. Charley never slowed his pace. He reached the smoldering Oak tree and began to dig furiously. He found nothing! It did not mat-

In the field behind this old home was the tree struck by lightning disclosing a fruit jar filled with money. The home is now private property and close to total ruin.

ter where he dug his holes, the shovel came up empty. Charley screamed into the howling wind. *"I have nothing left and now I'm going to lose that too!"*

In his anger, he threw the shovel with all his might at the burning Oak. Cursing his luck, he held the pick between his work-hardened hands and hurled it with all his might. The beveled edge of the pick struck the burning Oak dead on splitting the trunk open to reveal an old mason fruit jar.

Charley reached into the trunk of the tree and grabbed the jar. He never looked at its contents, nor did he really care what was inside. The jar was just something to peak curiosity, but not in a storm of this magnitude.

Charley returned to the house soaking wet and covered in mud. Bess scolded Charley as he stomped into her kitchen for going out into the storm. She feared he might contract pneumonia and leave her a widow as well as losing their home. Charley said nothing; he just placed the jar on the table and turned to wash his hands.

Before he could finish washing, he heard Bess yell in a quivering voice. "Lord in heaven!" Charley whirled in his tracks to see his Bess fall to the floor in a faint. She had taken the lid off the jar and, to his amazement...it was filled with money!

The theory that ghosts will sometimes show themselves in order to help those in need is still strong among believers of the paranormal. *Do you believe?*

THE RABBIT AND THE TOADSTOOLS

(Dare County)

Traveling east down Highway 64 in North Carolina, you will find yourself crossing the long bridge of the Croatan Sound and onto the shores of Roanoke Island. Some years ago, very close to the bridge was a very nice campground named Sandpiper's Trace. It was beautiful! Thousands of families came from far and near to stay here and drink in the beauty of its surroundings. This campground offered amenities for the children as well as adults with a boat ramp for fishing and a pier. The water was deep enough for swimming for all ages. It was truly a camper's delight. Many families kept their campers and trailers in storage there year round with some older couples opting to live on the premises.

The winters were mild and the beauty never diminished even during the winter months. The town of Manteo was only a few miles down the road when the residents needed to get groceries and do their shopping. There are many fine restaurants nearby and for those who desire more, a short trip across the next bridge are the Outer Banks.

The Outer Banks of North Carolina have ghost stories that begin from some of the first settlers coming to the islands. These stories are known around the world wherever you find the avid ghost hunter or researcher of the paranormal. Here on Roanoke Island the names of Sir Walter Raleigh, Virginia Dare, and the Croatan Indians are everyday names and the history that follows them. The disappearance of Virginia Dare is still one of the most investigated stories in the annals of American history; she was the first English child born in the New World. The only clue to the mystery was a single word carved into a tree, "CROATOAN." No other clues were found to tell what had happened to her or the other settlers who disappeared with her.

You will find tales of sea angels, the grey man that warns of impending disaster, and even the ghost light ships, but the tales that miss the press are in the everyday life of the residents. Roanoke Island has a magic and life of its own that few have experienced. To some, the stories may seem trivial and yet you wonder how can these things happen without the existence of another realm of reality.

Jeanette came to live at Sandpiper's Trace in the early 1980s. She and her husband had camped there for a few years and decided they wanted to stay year round. Her husband began working for the owner of the campground as maintenance and security. This gave them some income and allowed them to live as they chose very happily. Jeanette and her husband were very fond of the wildlife in the area and were always protecting the little animals in any way they could. Her husband was seen on more than one occasion feeding wild squirrels from his knee while sitting beneath the shade of the trees. They never attempted to bite him and always seemed to be gentle. Perhaps they were aware he would never try to hurt them.

During the day, while her husband was working, Jeanette roamed the campground and the edge of the wooded areas looking at the marvels of nature and finding herself at peace. She took many pictures of the wildlife and the flora of the area as well as the waters surrounding the island. She found unusual shaped trees that had been twisted from high winds and hurricanes over the years. Some reminded her of the trees from the Brother's Grimm tales.

Early one afternoon she sat in a lawn chair by their trailer and noticed at the edge of the woods a wonderful sight. She was quick to realize what a great photograph it would make. Carefully she rose from her seat and reached for her camera just inside the door. Aiming carefully, she snapped several pictures of a rabbit sitting among some of the prettiest toadstools she had ever seen. There were all sizes and the rabbit was enjoying his meal of the grass around them. No sooner than the click of the shutter was heard, the rabbit left his meal and scampered back into the forest.

Her husband came home from work about 5 o'clock in the evening and she told him about the picture she had taken that day. He told her it sounded like it would be a good picture and they would get the film processed as soon as possible. The weekend came and they went into Manteo for groceries and some shopping. While they were there, she dropped the film off to be developed at a local store and returned later to pick it up. Jeanette was excited to see the photographs she had taken. She opened the packet, examining each photograph, but to her dismay, the pictures of the rabbit and the toadstools were not there. The area she had snapped was definitely there as well as everything that had been close to the rabbit and the toadstools, and yet there was no rabbit or toadstools! She exclaimed to her husband that she knows she did not take a picture of something that wasn't there. He was in dismay also because she was not prone to telling lies of any kind. To look at the pictures, you would realize quickly that the person taking the picture is seeing more than what was produced on the film. The camera was not malfunctioning and the film was fresh. The gentleman at the camera shop explained that if the film had been bad he would have known right away. In his words, "There was nothing wrong with that film!"

Jeanette puzzled over this for awhile and then put the thought to the back of her mind in her box of memories. A few years later came the time Sandpiper's Trace had been sold to some developers. Jeanette and her husband sold their trailer and purchased a single, wide, two-bedroom mobile home to live in while at the beach. This new home was located in Old Kitty Hawk, within a short walking distance of the water. In the yard stood a large weeping willow that provided nice shade. She gained employment at a local restaurant while her husband began work in a warehouse in Nag's Head. On her days off, she worked in the yard with her flowers and visited with neighbors, enjoying the good life. One morning she noticed an unusual amount of small birds playing in the yard. They were around her flowers and the trees as well as her neighbor's yard close to her back door. She watched for awhile and then returned to her housework. When she looked out into the yard again, they were gone. Jeanette remarked to her husband what she had seen and they talked about what they looked like for she had never seen any like them. Her husband thought it might be some kind of Finch assuming this by their size and color. She did not see them again for a couple of days. A few days later she saw them again for the third time. She watched them for a while and then they flew into the yard of her neighbor across the road. Grabbing her camera she walked across the road and took several photographs of the little birds. They did not seem shy, or scare easily so she was assured of some good pictures.

Later in the day her husband arrived home from work and they went into Manteo to have the pictures developed. Opening the packet, they found not one bird in any of the photographs. No one has ever been able to explain this and, yes, she was not the only person to see these beautiful little birds.

When I investigated the site where Jeanette was living when the photographs were taken, I discovered her home as well as the other homes close by have been replaced with a new fire station for the Kitty Hawk community.

Chapter Seven:

LINGERING SPIRITS

A GHOSTLY PATH

(Gates County)

The Sand Banks is an area located just below the Virginia state line belonging to Gates County, North Carolina. The area is well known for its unusual sand content. If you are walking barefoot on this type of sand, the soles of your feet turn black. The texture of the sand is such that it is unusually fine in consistency. Nearly white on its surface, it is mixed with fine particles of pure black sand. This soil is excellent for the growth of plants, which is usually the contrary for plants. The sand particles are nearly as fine as powder. The wooded areas here are choked with briars and weeds of all shapes, sizes, and descriptions, some bearing wild berries that the local wildlife thrives on. Anywhere you travel in the area you are sure to leave some sign of where you have been and the direction you were traveling.

Close to the main highway that leads to Virginia is a very quaint country church. It was founded and built by the residents of the Sand Banks. At one time, there was a small one-room school that sat in the shade of the trees in the old churchyard. The school has long since been removed and a cemetery now fills the area where it once stood. This churchyard also has stories to tell.

The residents of this part of Gates County are no strangers to unearthly travelers. People visiting the area have also experienced the unexpected throughout the years. The roads here were not always paved and when the rains came, many times you would drive as far as you were able and then travel by foot for the rest of your destination. The sand upon the roads was very deep and one would easily compare these roads to driving on a beach. Plots of land were cleared for farming with many farms tucked neatly away from view back into the wooded areas. Whether you are walking, riding, or just enjoying yourself at home, the spirits of the dead walk among these people.

Myrtle was a child of the Sand Banks. Reared in the days of the Great Depression, she came from a very large family and had many friends. Her family lived close to a small village named Eure Station. This was the closest point for the residents to catch a train, enjoy traveling shows, or just gather family needs. It was a great place for friends to visit also. They came to hear music from such famous people as Chet Atkins and the Carter Family. It was just a few miles walking distance from their home. Nearby their grand-parents had a small farm and even at an early age the children would take a path through the woods to reach their home. It was much shorter than going by way of the road. The path from the farm ran down through the woods, across the railroad tracks, and eventually divided into a Y. Your destination depended on which route you were taking. It was not unusual to travel this path at all times of the day or night. Children of this area were accustomed to traveling alone or in pairs and held no fear of man or beast.

Seeing is Believing

Early one afternoon a friend of Myrtle's father stopped in for a visit. The two men sat and talked for awhile before his friend decided he would tell her father of what had happened to him. He told Myrtle's father not to let the children walk the path anymore alone, especially around dusk or after dark when the moon was full. Myrtle's father inquired about the reason for his statement. With close to fear in his eyes, the friend continued his story.

Though it's been widened for access to farming fields, remnants of the original path are still here.

"I left the farm close to dark yesterday evening and was heading up the path coming to your house. It was still light enough to see good and I was trying to get here before dark. Normally this time of year, it is a little muggy traveling through there and you really don't pay much attention to it. Yesterday when I got close to where the lane branches, I started to get really uncomfortable. I didn't understand why, but the feeling wouldn't leave me alone. When I got close to the 'Y,' a man I've never seen before stepped out of the woods ahead of me. It shook me at first because of the feeling I had. I relaxed a bit and took notice of him. He wore a white shirt, suspenders, and dark pants. Then I realized I couldn't see his feet. I decided to follow him and see where he was going. He stayed just far enough ahead of me to where I couldn't catch him. His stride was equal to mine the whole time. I followed him up the path and then he turned and walked up the path toward your house, so I kept following him. Pretty soon, we came to a small turn in the path, but before he reached it, he disappeared right in front of me. It didn't strike me up till then, but the whole time you could look right through him. I don't want anything to happen to the young'uns so I thought I might tell you about it."

Myrtle's father nodded his head in agreement, but made no comment on what his friend had witnessed. The following day, he told his family that he did not want them walking the path close to dark anymore. In this date and age, when a parent or grown person told you something to do, you did not question it; you just obeyed. He did tell Myrtle's mother what he had been told because she also traveled the same path regularly. It did not take long for the children to get the full story of their father's reason for not telling them. They obeyed their father and traveled the lane only in the light of day. If they stayed too long at the grandparent's house, they usually just spent the night with them.

It was only a few short months after the reported sighting of the ghost that the threat seemed to be gone and everything returned to normal. Nobody sighted the ghostly figure again and they began to walk the lane as they had done before.

Myrtle and one of her sisters had not long passed over the railroad tracks returning from her grandparent's farm. They walked down the lane talking and laughing, paying little attention to their surroundings. It was near dark with the light of day fading quickly before them. Shortly before reaching the fork in the lane, a man stepped out of the edge of the woods in front of them He seemed oblivious to their presence and started walking toward where the lane branches. He was wearing a white shirt with suspenders, dark trousers, and black shoes. They stopped and watched him, fear gripping their hearts. He was a large man and they could see the woods right *through* him. The fear that chilled them to the bone was seeing he had no head! Seconds after the ghostly image had entered the path, he disappeared before their eyes.

The children recalled the incident for their father when they reached home. It became evident that there was more than one ghost on the path they knew so well. The children, as well as the adults, never used the path again except in the full light of day.

An Unknown Entity

The family moved several times in their early years. Myrtle's father rented a home large enough for his family deeper into the Sand Banks. On this side of the Sand Banks, when darkness fell, it was pitch black. The moon did not shine through the trees and without a light you could not see your hand in front of your face. Her father worked nights at the shipyard in Norfolk, Virginia, and left early each day to be able to meet someone to ride to work with.

Myrtle's mother was a stouthearted woman and could not be scared easily. They moved into the new home settling in nicely. It was a very large, two-story home in good condition and seemed to be just what they wanted. She kissed her husband and sent him off to work that evening. The family unpacked all they owned trying to have everything prepared for when their father returned from work the next morning. They all went to bed early that evening tired from the effort of moving to a new home.

During the course of the night, something happened in their new home. Myrtle's mother sat the rest of the night waiting for her husband to return from work. She had been up most of the night and found it difficult to wait much longer for his return. Immediately upon his arrival, she told him they had to move. Today! She said she would not spend another night within the walls of that house. Her husband said they could not move that day because they had no place to go. She immediately told him, "Then you will stay here alone. I will not stay here another night and neither will any of my children."

Myrtle's mother never said what happened during the night and refused to discuss it with anyone, not even her family. It was very clear something in the house built in the Sand Banks had frightened her badly and is still a mystery to this day. It appears we may never know.

Further reports of the two apparitions along the path being sighted have not been found and the people of the area will change the subject if you ask them about the ghosts of Eure Station.

Though the old mill house is no longer standing, here you will find the millpond that lies directly against what was once the original road used for transporting grains to the mill for processing.

HARE'S MILL

(Hertford County)

Near the town of Winton, North Carolina, is an old gristmill. The history of this mill goes back to the 1740s when it was first built. A town or area having a gristmill was a sign of permanence. Mill owners usually possessed large capital and political clout, and were usually slave owners who trained their slaves to become millers. The original owners of Hare's Mill were Job Rogers and Jonathon Gilbert, both men of considerable influence. The mill was a gathering place for residents and a place to have their corn and wheat ground for consumption and feed for their animals.

The millpond is a spectacular site. It is a step backward into time. The beauty of the Cyprus trees and still quiet waters are almost breathtaking. There are few places that can instill a feeling of genuine tranquility as this mill does. There were hundreds of buildings and farms destroyed during the Civil War in this area, but Hare's Mill was never touched. It stands today as it did when it was built. The fishing in the pond is excellent and the gentle breezes that flow through the trees is still to be enjoyed as they did when the mill was in its glory.

To see the mill now, you might find it hard to associate it with slavery. The black slaves worked the mill and kept everything to the satisfaction of the slave owners. This was the slave owners' livelihood and the slaves were still slaves without hope of one day gaining freedom. In any instance, there were times when a slave died of misfortune, heartache, and a hundred other reasons, including murder. It is here we find that through the years Hare's Mill carried a secret to the outside world.

Early in North Carolina history, lawmakers made it illegal for slaves to own drums. They believed it was one of the ways they had of rebelling against slave owners. The drums could be used to pass messages and possibly make plans for attacks on their masters or to try and escape. Regardless of what the slave master thought, he had little knowledge that the drums were not only for the slaves' religious ceremonies, but also a form of entertainment for them.

Drumming to His Own Beat

On a hot summer night two men from Cofield, North Carolina, were walking the road from Cofield to Winton. They were young men without a care to bother them. They walked briskly along the road, talking and laughing as good friends will. As they approached the bridge at Hare's Mill, they decided to sit on the rail of the bridge and rest before continuing their journey. The moon hung low over the millpond, illuminating it with its golden light and casting eerie shadows across the waters. The two men dreamed of the day when they would have their own home and desired a pond that looked just as Hare's Mill did that night. After some minutes, they stopped talking to each other and just admired the beauty of the millpond. Very lightly, almost imperceptible at first, they heard the rhythm of a single drum in the distance. They listened carefully trying to figure out which direction it was coming from. It seemed to be coming from every direction, but not all at once. The sound of the drum never increased, and still it came from everywhere at once. They knew it did not sound like any drum they had ever heard and it was obvious by the sound it was beaten by hand.

The millpond began to take on a quality that was disturbing to them. The water no longer shimmered in the moonlight and the Cyprus trees began to take on a quality not unlike seeing the negative of a photograph. The two young men suddenly wanted to be anywhere but the bridge at Grist Mill. They started hastily back on the road to Winton. Within minutes, they stopped in their tracks, staring at the wooded road before them. In the moonlight, walking towards them, was a black man with no shoes. The shirt draped across his thin shoulders was not of this time. His trousers were almost rags about his ankles. They agreed something about the man was not right. They both had a feeling of foreboding as they watched him approach. The ghostly figure moved ever closer to them, as they seemed frozen in their tracks. The time passed slowly and quickly in the same breath. They could now see the face of the black apparition and found a look of shear terror on his face. They realized everything behind him could be seen in the moonlight through his body. The man was not much more than a misty vapor.

Terrified at the sight coming toward them, they were finally able to turn from the ghost and run for their lives. The sound of the drum faded from their ears as they raced for home. After what seemed like an eternity, they finally reached home and collapsed on the front porch gasping for breath.

A Slave's Tragic End

The next day the young men relayed the story of their experience to one of their uncles. He frowned and said he had never heard of anything like that happening around the old mill, but he would ask around and let them know.

A week later the uncle took the boys over to an old woman's house. She declared herself to be a root doctor. The house appeared as though it would fall down about their ears as they entered the front door. In their young eyes, no one could be as old as she appeared to be. She cackled a toothless laugh and told the boys her name was Miss Sally. "Ever body here bouts knows Miss Sally," she laughed again. She told the boys she knew what they had come to her home for and then ordered them to sit down. Her chocolate brown eyes narrowed almost to a slit as she spoke. Her voice was barely audible in the tiny room.

She sat close before a lighted fireplace even though the temperature outside was sultry hot. She began to speak in a voice that bothered the young men, but they listened with great interest.

"You been over bout the mill. Dat place ain't nowhere to be for a black man. You seen him close to da bridge, das where he come up dead. Dat was dat boy Jeeter. He was young like you is when dey did him. Yep, he was drown in the water right dere by da bridge for all folks to see. What he done was made him a new drum. Said no man tell him what he cain't have. Well, it costs him his life and da folks what done it never paid for dat life. So he come back ever chance he gits and you be the first to see him in years. Stay way from da bridge and you be all right."

With that said, she rose from her chair and walked out of the back door, leaving them to wonder if her story was true. Little did the boys have any idea that Jeeter was her grandfather.

The boy's uncle led them out of the house and back down the road. He told them that if anybody knew what they saw it would be her. Miss Sally's house was torn down many years ago, but there are still those who swear they have heard the drum at Hare's Mill.

THE STEEL MILL

(Halifax County)

Along the banks of the Tar River, Howell Steel Service operated for many years. The owner was always very good to his employees and anyone who worked for him seemed well satisfied with his job. Howell Steel Service is no longer in business and has been gone for many years, but we are left to wonder if some of its employees are still at their job.

During the Civil War, a brick mill was located at this site. Several entrances to the areas where the bricks were baked and stored

can still be seen on the property. These tunnels run beneath the mill and are small by some standards. The ceilings are arched and the floors are made entirely of handmade brick.

In 1983, Micheal was working as a steel fabricator/welder for Howell Steel. He had worked at his position for two years and was very happy with his job. There were times when parts ran low and he would have to fabricate the parts for the huge I beams himself. He would cut the plates, mark and drill the holes, and return to his work area.

The area where the drill press stood was next to the room where the extra parts or the parts already prepared for the beams were kept. From his work area, this drill press could be seen without difficulty.

On a lazy summer afternoon he received a work order for an I-beam that had to be rushed for shipping. He noticed there were no parts on the beam and the drawing called for specialized plating. Quickly he gathered his drawing and all the necessary tools to cut, layout, and drill the necessary pieces of steel for the beam. His time was limited.

Micheal walked from his work area and headed for the drill press. As he passed through the first set of steel rollers, he looked over at the drill press and found someone already working there with a large amount of plating in front of him. He thought quickly. Micheal headed in the other direction and brought back a large, heavy hand drill with a magnetic base to drill holes for his plates. He knew he did not have the time to wait for the man on the drill press to finish.

After he had drilled less than three holes in the first plate, his supervisor came to check his progress. Puzzled, his supervisor asked him why he was drilling the holes by hand. Micheal told him there was another worker already on the drill press working on a large amount of plating and he could not wait for the man to finish.

Thirty feet from the entrance of this warehouse stood the drill press for fabricating parts. It was here that a ghost was seen performing his job on many occasions by more than one person. This steel mill is no longer in operation.

The supervisor looked over at the press and told Micheal that there was no one there and no plates either. Micheal looked over and was mildly surprised. It was hard to understand how the man had either finished so quickly or had just stopped working on the plates. His supervisor already knew there was not a man available for any of the drill or punch press work. He asked Micheal what the man looked like.

Micheal described the man as being in his fifties, stocky built, balding, and blue coveralls. His supervisor chuckled deep within his chest, then grinned as he spoke.

"Congratulations... You have just met Walter. He used to work here up until about five years ago. He ran the drill press for all the parts coming through the mill. Walter had a heart attack while he was working some parts and fell dead. You look a little shocked, but don't worry, a lot of us get to see Walter and we got used to it."

With that being said, the supervisor walked away, leaving Micheal to his work. Micheal finished drilling the parts by hand. From that day on, as he passed the drill press, Micheal always wondered if he was alone or if Walter was going to come back to finish his work.

THE TRESTLE

(Hertford County)

The railroad was an important supplier for the town of Ahoskie even as far as the late 1960s. It transported goods and hauled freight from this town. If a farmer or anyone needed grain or wheat straw for their animals, they came to the train station to make their purchases. The variety of these goods was many and well needed by the residents here.

Leaving the station and heading south, the tracks will take you down by the old peanut processing plant and a well-known supplier for building materials. Both of these companies

The overhead pass where the vision of an apparition walking the tracks was sighted.

used the railway system for many years before it was no longer in use. If you stand on the tracks and gaze southward, where the old trestle stood, you have a clear view. There are no obstructions of any kind with a line of sight all the way to the rolling curve running through an open field.

A small bridge, or overpass, is located a short distance from the peanut plant. We shall call our friend "D" for the sake of this story. D had started to cross the bridge one hot sultry afternoon in July. Just as he came to the center of the bridge, he looked down the railroad tracks to his left. There he saw a medium height black

man in old clothing walking just off the trestle headed for the town limits. There was a certain something about this man that did not fit. He seemed to be in a haze of some kind. Thinking that it may be heat coming off of the tracks causing his appearance to be less than normal, D left the bridge and went down onto the tracks. Once there he could see nothing but the train trestle. There was no man of any kind to be seen. Satisfied he went back onto the bridge to continue his journey. Reaching the center of the bridge once more, he looked to his left and the thin black man was there again. He always looked to be walking and D could see his legs moving with every stride. The problem was the man never made forward progress...he always walked in the same place.

Immediately D ran back to the end of the bridge and went below onto the tracks, peering toward the trestle. Again, the man was nowhere to be found.

Back on the bridge once more, he stood watching the black man trying to walk the railroad tracks. His head and hands were always hazy to D's sight, but the clothing, even with the haze, was distinctive. His suspenders stood in contrast to the white of his shirt. The dark brown trousers and black shoes also could be seen with little effort.

Straining to see the black man's face was an exercise in futility. The more his eyes focused on the face and torso of the black man, the less he was able to see. When D did not concentrate on him, the black man became much clearer.

D tried to see him down on the tracks once more. At this time, he started to have reservations about the man. Caution dictated not to get too curious. D temporarily ignored these feelings, as he headed down the tracks toward the point where he had seen the black man traveling. The closer he got to the point, the more overpowering was the feeling of apprehension. Reaching the halfway point, D lost his nerve and turned back to the bridge. Soon he had reached the bridge and climbed the hill to walk back to the center. D turned to his left and once again saw the black man walking in the exact same spot as before.

D never forgot that hot summer day in July. Later, he remembered even more what he had seen while walking the tracks from the trestle. To this day he swears to what he witnessed and cannot be shaken from his story. The tracks are no longer in use now, but it gives you cause to wonder if the black man D had seen is still trying to make his journey complete.

A ONE-ROOM SCHOOL

(Hertford County)

In the 1960s, Miss Jessie Vann lived a mile down what is known as Vann Road in Brantley's Grove, North Carolina. Located three miles outside of the Ahoskie city limits makes it very easy to locate for those of a curious nature. This road remained unpaved right on up through the early 1980s. During hot summers when little rain fell, this road was nearly a dust bowl for those who found it necessary to travel here. At the very end of the road is a small creek tucked neatly back into a wooded area.

As a child, I traveled this road often, riding my bike with my friends. We would ride this road looking at the fields and doing our best to find an opportunity for a new adventure. There were times we would find a snake or two for some excitement, but more often than not it would remain just another very hot trip down a long, dusty, dirt road.

For a few years we traveled this road and the result was always the same. We would always find ourselves visiting Miss Jessie and sitting on her porch for awhile talking. We liked visiting with her because we knew she would have something sweet for us to eat. We ate fresh figs from her trees as well as apples and pears. When she did her canning of fruit for the year, we were always assured of a dry peach cake or fresh apple pie.

Miss Jessie often told us stories of when she was young and had her entire family still with her. She had an easy laugh and her eyes laughed with her. It was not hard to understand how very much she enjoyed life even at the doorway of old age. She loved children of all ages and it radiated from her face whenever you came to see her. She forever had a kind word and you never went away hungry.

School came to an end and we were out for the summer break. I knew I would be able to get a lot of good things to eat by visiting Miss Jessie on a regular basis. I had a plan and I carried it through.

Early one Saturday morning I made my way down the dusty road to her house. Before I even had the opportunity to knock on her door, she suddenly appeared, smiling broadly. "What can I do for you, little man?" she asked.

Before I could answer, she opened the screen door wide and stepped out onto the porch. "I come to see if I could help you with anything," I boldly announced to her. I was so small that all she could do was grin and chuckle to herself. She stood straight of back and looked down at me. "Okay, I believe I have just the thing. You sit in that chair and I'll be back in a minute."

I sat in the oversized rocking chair on her front porch and waited for her return. When the screen door opened again, she had a plate with a few cookies and two glasses of cold well water.

As she sat down in the swing next to the chair, she made a noisy exhale as many people do when they are tired and close to the end. "This is a little job I think you can handle without no problem. Now you sit there and I'll tell you a story. This ain't no regular story like you find in a book, but now that don't mean it ain't so you understand."

I nodded and listened to her soothing voice.

"That old one-room schoolhouse up yonder didn't always look like it does now. Me and my sister went to school there and I graduated from that school. I agree it don't look like much, but we had a good teacher and she was smart as a whip. I learned everything from my ABCs to Algebra in that little building.

Back in those days men didn't want us women knowing too much about their business so they were not so agreeable about girls going to school. We went anyhow because my Momma ruled this roost. Daddy didn't say a word...he just got his hat and went to the store at the end of the road for a spell.

Miss Suzy taught the school there. She never did marry nobody and I heard tell that nobody come to see her either. That's neither here nor there, but I just thought I'd tell you. Everyday we would put

The one-room schoolhouse near the home of Miss Jessie Vann was reported to be haunted by the spirit of a nine-year-old little girl who died of influenza in the early 1900s. The child was reported to be blond and slim. A weak little smile shows on her face as she watches you.

on our good clothes and walk down to the school for the day. This close to the house Momma didn't bother to pack no dinner. You just come to eat when they let you out for dinner. Durin' the winter, we had a wood stove in there bout the middle of the room to keep us warm. It put out good heat best as I remember. Come to think of it I never seen a wood burner that didn't heat up the place good.

There were two or three folks that got the wood for us, and my Daddy was one of them. They took turns bringing it you understand. Daddy never showed his self when he come to the school cause he didn't want to disturb the teacher. Sis didn't see him, but I seen him every time he come.

I still remember Daddy going to Ahoskie just to get us a chalkboard to write on. I still got the first pen he gimme too."

I watched Miss Jessie as she told her story... The light in her eyes shone as if she was reliving every minute of it.

"When I was about ten or so, one of the little girls in my school came down with the flu. She was out of school for a long time and the grown folks didn't say much about her when the young'uns were in the room. We kept up with our schoolwork and right before Christmas we got word the little girl had passed away. We never expected nothin' like that, but we also knew you didn't question the Lord's work. I know I'm getting old and I cain't for the life of me remember that child's name. Fore this is over it'll come to me. Your Grandma knew her folks.

We went on about our business, and when the time come I was old enough to get married, I done it and I been here on this old farm ever since. Worked hard, had children of my own, and tended Momma and Daddy when they got old and passed on. Buried my husband too time it was over.

Looks like I'm straying a little bit. That young girl that got the flu and died won't never forgot by none of us. We didn't linger on it mind you, but she was remembered well.

Me and my husband started to go to town and get a few groceries one Saturday morning. Fact is, it was about the same time as it is now. We got into that old piece of car he bought from a fella from Gates County or somewhere, and off we went down the path and headed for Hoskie. I never did like that car cause it smelled like a cigar all the time.

We stayed most of the day and just before we got home I started to feel a little funny. It was like my neck hair had a mind of its own. I got a cold shiver run down my back and everything looked a little different to me for a minute.

It was close to then that we came up on the little schoolhouse. I tell you good as I sit here I seen that little girl I told you about standing close to the door. I know it was her and I'd swear to it. Fast as I seen her, she popped back around the corner and disappeared clean as a whistle. When she done that, I felt alright again. I didn't say nothing to my husband...I just let it go for then. I looked over at my husband and he had the strangest look on his face, but he won't say a word either. Don't know if he seen her too, but if he didn't he sure acted like something was out of place.

Sunday morning I got up to go to church. Just like I used to before I got so I cain't half walk. Got myself ready and called my husband from the yard. He come in sweatin' like a preacher with a full house. I asked him what in the world was wrong with him. He didn't waste no time. He told me he had been trying to catch one of dogs before they went to church. He run him down right close to the little schoolhouse. Just as he grabbed the deerhound's collar, he seen that little girl watchin' him from the back of the school. When he raised his head to get a good look, she disappeared from sight. That old dog come home on his own and hid under the porch for the rest of the evening. That was one time I didn't have an ounce of trouble getting' that old man of mine past the church doors.

Awhile later, probably about a year or so, I seen her again when I went to the field to get some peanuts for roasting. I stopped dead still and watched her for a few minutes. The more she looked at me, the more I wanted to run. But I couldn't cause my legs just won't go nowhere! Everything I had refused to move until she went back around the corner of the school.

I ran back to the house. Right by the school, the old well, and left the mail sittin' in the box. Never done that in my life. Never did again after that day. I went to the mailbox first, then down to the fields."

I heard her laugh loudly as if it was the funniest joke anyone could ever make.

"I have seen this girl at some of the strangest times. It has never been at a particular time like a ghost with good sense. She just pops up whenever she gets ready and scares the britches off you. She just stands there looking at you. She ain't never said nothin' and she don't try to come to you. But I am here to tell you she will make you want to go home a little quicker.

If you see a little blond headed girl when you go by there and it don't feel right to you, run with everything you got and get out of there. It ain't no place for little boys. I seen you and your friend lookin' inside the school. That's a good thing, but you never know when that girl might slip up on you. I don't want you to hurt yourself if she pops up in front of you."

We talked until she tired enough to take her nap. I left soon after I took her trash to the burn barrel and headed for home. When I passed the little school, I started getting the same feeling I always had. I always wanted to go in, but never by myself. I suppose her story was true and yet I had to find out for myself.

In the evening, my father returned from work and we sat in the front yard talking. The cool of the evening had settled in and everyone seemed relaxed. It was then that I told him of visiting Miss Jessie and told him the story she passed to me of the little girl.

My father sat and listened, saying nothing. He nodded now and then and looked out toward the peanut patch. When I finished, he nodded slightly and said he knew of the little girl. The story he had been told was told as truth and as far as he knew it was. While deer hunting near Miss Jessie's farm, he and his hunting partner had noticed the dogs would never go near the old school. Once, when it started to rain, he and his partner took shelter there, waiting for the rain to stop. They could never explain why, but they both walked in the rain and stood beneath the hog shelter instead of the roof of the old school until the rain stopped. My father shrugged his shoulders and said: "The place ain't never felt right to me."

Chapter Eight:

CROOKED GHOSTS

SEVEN SPRINGS

(Wayne County)

The word Prohibition still brings back many memories for the older citizens. This was a time when the young and old, rich and poor found it difficult to get or consume any alcoholic beverage. It was illegal to posses or drink in all the states. However, this did not deter Americans from finding and consuming their favorite drinks. From bathtub distilleries in the north to the moonshine stills of the Ozarks, whiskey could be found. The bold went so far as to smuggle whiskey in from Canada.

The citizens of our bigger cities like Chicago, New York, and Boston began to open speakeasies and other secret clubs to entertain themselves with dining, dancing, and, above all, good whiskey. Famous gangsters made their fortunes from these clubs as well as offering them protection for a good price. The money they made from the whiskey sold in these places amassed an amazing profit. Many times they cut, or dilute, the whiskey to double their profits. They became very adept at hiding their profession from the prying eyes and ears of the police and federal authorities. The number of corrupt political officials who became rich from the kickbacks from Prohibition sales is still unknown.

Over the years gangsters from the northern states made themselves famous with their own brand of justice. Most considered themselves above the law and traveled the country far and wide to obtain illegal whiskey. It did not take them long to discover that whiskey made in the southern states was not only easily obtainable, but some of the finest whiskey in the world. They soon made their way into the south and bartered for their whiskey.

Seven Springs, North Carolina, is located in Wayne County. It is the home for a modest ninety residents. The first home constructed here was in 1742 by William Whitfield, an English surveyor. It was soon after the Civil War ended that Seven Springs was given its name, which derived from the excellent waters of the natural springs. The Neuse River lays very close to the natural springs, but does not contribute to its waters. It was in this small community that the finest whiskey any state ever produced was distilled and distributed... *illegally*!

Seven Springs never grew like the towns around them, but the citizens seemed to prefer their way of life to the hustle and bustle of the towns nearby. During the days shortly after the Civil War, two small motels were built to accommodate travelers and businessmen. Famous gangsters, Al Capone, Legs Diamond, and Lucky Luciano, were just a few of the well-known names that came to Seven Springs to buy whiskey and spend a little time fishing. Other famous men came to visit also, but probably not to buy the whiskey. These men were former governors of the state. This was a place they could come and relax without worry. They ate well, slept soundly, and, above all for those in the business, placed their orders for the perfect whiskey. There were little or no reports of anything happening while they stayed at Seven Springs. This is why many wonder why the gangsters came back to haunt the area.

Alan lived close by Seven Springs and enjoyed the pleasures of being part of the community. He and his friends played by the shores of the Neuse River and camped at the Falls of the Neuse. He and a few of his closest friends decided to camp one evening at a small cove cut into the wooded area that offered good protection from the wind and would afford better cover if it should start to rain. Darkness came and the small fire crackled in the evening air. It gave a gentle warmth, just enough to keep them all from being chilled. In the distance, he could hear the waters of the Neuse as they made their way down stream. About 11 o'clock they all became very quiet. They heard the sound of an automobile making its way up the path to where they were camped. This was a problem, as they all knew the path was not wide enough for a car of any size to be coming that far up into the woods. They sat very quietly, listening intently for what would happen next. They looked to see the dim headlights of what appeared to be a Packard. Alan knew it was a Packard because his father collected antique cars. The fact still remained, though, that there was not enough room to drive a vehicle this close to where they camped. A cold chill ran through the boys as the phantom rolled to a stop thirty feet from where they sat. They watched as the large car door on the driver's side opened and a man stepped from the car. They could still hear the engine rumbling through the stillness.

The man was short and very well dressed. His clothing was vintage and the boys gasped as they realized they could see the trees right through him. As they watched, he appeared to be talking to someone they could not see. Suddenly his body jerked twice spasmodically and he fell to the ground. As he fell, he and the car slowly dissolved into nothing. It was as if it had never happened. Alan realized that while all of this was taking place he had not heard a single frog or cricket like they had been hearing all evening. Even now the silence was nearly deafening. The boys quickly gathered their things and ran for home.

Alan told his father what had happened by the Falls of the Neuse and his father told him the story he had heard when he was a child. He said his father heard of a man from the city that came to buy whiskey from a local moonshiner. The man from the city tried to get rough with the moonshiner. The ways of business for the moonshiner and the ways of doing business for the gangster did not meet in a happy union. The moonshiner shot the gangster and buried him by the Cliffs of the Neuse. There is nobody living that knows where the gangster is buried and if they did they would never say. The car disappeared in the night never to be seen. His father said many strange things happen by the cliffs. You can camp in certain places and find it very difficult to sleep because of strange noises. The noises are not anything the animals, woods, or water create. You can hear footsteps walk up to your tent or campfire and yet there is no one to be seen. Personal items disappear without signs of a visitor. Some say something has touched them in the night soon after a cold chill has descended upon them like a blanket of ice. Alan's grandfather told the tale of someone calling his name near the same cove Alan and his friends had shared the night before. The voice came from the river, and he never returned to camp there again.

The Cliffs of the Neuse is now a state park and is considered a very beautiful place to relax and enjoy life. The camping sites are numbered and the area that was once a haunted cove is Lot 7. There were some reports of unusual activity at Lot 7 as recently as 1993. You'll have to visit the site for yourself... Maybe you will see the phantom Packard and its unlucky driver.

THE WINDOW

(Gates County)

Gates County is the bearer of many strange tales. In the 1930s, one tale that stands out in the memories of some of its residents is bordering on the bizarre. Within every town, city, and rural area, criminal activity can and does take place. Some of these criminals are very crafty and almost impossible to catch with solid evidence to convict them in a court of law.

There was a time in our country when vigilantes were not only not unheard of, but were also quietly praised for their work. A community at times held more than a slight hand in apprehending the criminal or doling out their own brand of justice. In this story, the circumstances surrounding the latter evidence may possibly be true; however, only one person was willing to come forth with the story and she has been granted anonymity from the tale...

As a teenager, I visited the original house where this murder had taken place. At the time the house still stood with bare unpainted wood just a few feet off the dirt road. It stood forlorn and empty with an air of foreboding. I never had a desire to enter or approach the house to see the bloodstains upon the windows next to the front door. It was of an old style with rectangular panes placed on either side for anyone to be seen standing on the covered front porch. There were two floors to the house and the rooms were small judging from the outside dimensions. From the road you could still see the fireplace in the sitting room. Its bare walls and broken pieces of furniture littered about the floor stood as silent witnesses to a house nobody wanted.

He's Left His Blood

As the tale goes, a man and his wife lived in this home for several years. He was a large burly man who was said to possess a lot of physical strength and a very ill temperament. The ladies and men around the community had witnessed the affect of the abuse he had inflicted on his wife. There were days when she was not seen at all, sometimes for several days, only to emerge from her home with fresh bruises and possibly bandages.

Her husband had earned himself a reputation in the area. He was not very well liked by anyone, but they did not mistreat him. Shortly after the couple moved into the home, neighbors and community residents began to find things being stolen from them. These were hard-working families that did not have very much and times were very hard for all of them. The sheriff had tried everything thing he knew to catch the thief and still the thief stayed one step ahead.

There came a time when everyone realized the man doing the stealing was undoubtedly the man nobody liked. The evidence was all there, but they still could not catch him in the act of stealing. The people of the community knew in their hearts he had committed other crimes as well.

Something happened that people of the area would not speak of and they gathered to meet with the sheriff and voice their complaints. They wanted the man out of their lives and if he could not get rid of this man they could.

It was said the sheriff and the Ku Klux Klan went to the man's house and ordered him to come out. He refused and began to shoot at them from an upstairs window. The sheriff and the Ku Klux Klan started shooting back and finally wounded the man. Trying to escape, the man made it to the stairs and fell. Bleeding from several wounds, he splattered blood on the stairs and one of the windows at the front door when he hit the bottom of the stairs. He crawled to the sitting room and worked his way up into the chimney trying to escape. Being a large man he was soon trapped inside the chimney. The men broke into the house and followed the trail of blood into the sitting room. There they found him trapped in the fireplace with no way to escape them. He was dragged from the chimney and killed.

The house was rented out to other people not long after the killing had taken place. The new tenants never knew of the justice that had been served. A woman was hired to clean the house for the new tenants. The blood spatters on the flooring could not be removed at any costs. The blood spattered on the window next to the front door was scraped away and the window cleaned. The following day the blood was back on the window. The blood on the window always returned. Replace the window you say? The blood still returned!

Eventually they could not find anyone willing to live in the house. A haunting of any kind was never reported and the house eventually fell to the ground. A new house was never built on the property. The land sits now as a reminder for those who knew what happened here. The question remains as to whether or not the spirit of the criminal still remains with the property. That is for you to decide.

SOOKIE FIELD

(Northampton County)

In many regions throughout the world, farming is the way of life for millions of people. These hard-working individuals and their families feed the world. They are valued members of the communities and not very often thought of in the cities. Mr. Glover was just such a farmer. He was not a remarkable man and yet everyone in his community knew him well and what his profession was.

In the 1960s, he was able to purchase a piece of land he had wanted to add to his own farm for a very long time. He was a man of sensibility and not given to believing the tales of people he considered not being of the same mind as himself. Mr. Glover did not believe in ghosts, or witches, or anything that goes bump in the night. The thought of something happening to someone without seeing him or her was absolutely impossible! Then the land and all the ghostly tales and curses came to him at a very reasonable price, so he was quick to purchase it.

Mr. Glover was thrifty with a dollar to say the least. To say the most he was bordering on miserly, but he was happy and those who knew him had no complaints about their neighbor. In a time of need for his fellow man, he could be counted on to help. The land he wanted so badly had a tainted reputation. The growing of crops was not difficult on this land, but timing was everything whenever you wanted to plow, plant, or harvest.

Sookie Field is located on the North Carolina/Virginia border. The land is rich for farming and the yield for crops has always been very good. A half-mile down the dirt road from the Sookie Field is a short bridge over a swift running creek where the wildlife used to come and drink often...that is until Sookie took her life by hanging herself from this bridge.

Witchery Done Him In

In or about 1935, a young farmer and his wife sharecropped a small farm until he was able to save enough money to buy it. This farm yielded good crops and soon he was able to build a house for himself and his three children. They were very happy with their lives and things changed for them all. He no longer had to scrimp and save every dime to make ends meet and there was always a bounty of food upon his table. Whenever the young farmer went into the nearest town for seed or any other supplies, Sookie would seek him out and try to get the farmer to leave his wife for her. She would tell him what a wonderful wife she would be and he would always be happy as long as he stayed with her. Desperately in love, she would do anything to have him for her own. The young farmer was not all that she desired, though. Sookie wanted his farm far more than she wanted him, but she could not farm the land herself.

The young farmer feared her because she was known to be a witch and the people of the community shied away from her as much as possible. A story had gone about the county years before that she was responsible for the death of her husband even though they could not prove it. Everyone, including law enforcement, believed her to be a witch and did everything they could to not anger her for fear of her powers of witchcraft.

The young farmer went into town early one afternoon to buy seed to plant his new crops. When he came out onto the sidewalk, Sookie seemed to appear from nowhere standing nearly at his side. With a look in her eyes that would frighten any man, she told him that within the year he would be her husband. With this being said, she walked away and down the street. The young farmer felt a cold chill race down his spine. He hurried home to his wife and children, praying they were all safe.

When he arrived home, everything was normal and his wife smiled sweetly at him. The nights became long and he did not sleep well. Sookie's words rang in his ears. It mattered not what he tried to do; he heard her voice as though she was close by.

For several months, he did not see Sookie nor did anyone else. It was a blessing and a time of fear in the same breath. In the middle of the night the young farmer's middle child was found on the floor of his room with a raging fever. The farmer sent word for the doctor to come as quickly as he could for the child seemed to be close to death. The doctor was never able to cool the fevered brow of the child and three days later the farmer's son was dead. Neither the doctor nor his colleagues could find any reason for the sudden fever. There was no evidence of a snakebite, or any kind of insect to make this possible. The child had eaten the same meal the rest of the family had eaten and was in a very good mood when he was put to bed. Still the fever ravaged his small body until death came to him.

One week later, the young farmer spotted Sookie standing at the edge of his field behind the house. She smiled a vicious little smile and held up one finger for him to see. Almost as quick as the blink of an eye she was gone. The young farmer dropped the reins for the mule he was using to plow the field and ran for his house. He ran inside and found his youngest child, a daughter, choking. He tried everything he knew and was not able to save her. She died in his arms within minutes. The doctor again could not find a reason for this. There was nothing found in her throat to choke on and her stomach showed she had not eaten that morning. The funeral for the second child was held on a Sunday afternoon. The young farmer spotted Sookie standing a distance away from the funeral procession holding up two fingers. The young farmer started toward her and then watched her vanish before his eyes. No one else saw her, but he saw her and nearly fell into a rage.

When the funeral had ended and all visitors had gone home, the young farmer left his home and went to Sookie's house. He was afraid of her, but more afraid of losing anymore of his family. She came to the door and listened to what he had to say. It was then she told him she had nothing to do with what had happened to his family and come what may, they would marry by the following spring.

Christmas was sad for them that year. They missed the children, but tried their best to make the last child's Christmas a happy one. On Christmas morning, the child could not be awakened from his sleep. The young farmer ran for the doctor and came back home shaking with the cold. Again the doctor could find no cause to this. Everything he tried was to no avail; the child continued to sleep. The good doctor began to spend his nights at the farmer's home in hopes that h e could find a way to bring this child back to them. At the end of March, the child succumbed to death, never opening his eyes or muttering a single word. The wife blamed Sookie and promised her death would be as cruel as what she dealt. This was not to be. The young farmer's wife was found a week later and the court ruled it as suicide.

Everyone knew she would have never done anything to herself. She was a woman with pride and would fight to the death for what she believed to be right and her hatred for Sookie had become well known throughout the county. Sookie knew her way to the farmer and his farm was free and clear for her to take. She came to the farmer's house during the night. It was never said what happened then, but spring came...and Sookie became a new bride with a prosperous farm.

She moved in before they were married and threw out everything that had ever belonged to his family. She treated the young farmer badly and demanded more and more of him as time went on. He began to look seriously ill, but refused help from anyone. This delighted Sookie for soon the farm and his money would be hers. She had already made plans to hire someone to work the farm when he was gone. She did not have long to wait. Within two years of the marriage, the young farmer died of exhaustion — and Sookie inherited everything!

The young farmer had been very well thought of in the town. Sookie came to town one afternoon and the townspeople gathered around her. She was told she would pay for what she had done to the young farmer and others in the community. She hissed at the crowd and told them they would never harm her and anyone who ever tried to live on her farm would regret it. She ran home and tried to think of a way to protect herself. It was to no avail. Within a few days, many people gathered in front of her house and demanded she come out. She refused and they tried to storm the farmhouse with the intention of dragging her from her home and banishing her from the county. Sookie screamed from the front window, *"Nobody will ever live in **my** house!"* This being said she escaped from the back of the house and ran for the bridge. When the townspeople arrived, she had hanged herself from the bridge rather than face the angry mob.

Cursed from Beyond the Grave?

Another family bought the farm and tried to stay in the house where Sookie had lived her final days. They reported instances of dishes being thrown at them with no one to be seen and howls from inside the home in the dead of night. Yet the final straw for them was this farmer watching his wife being strangled by unseen hands. The marks on her throat turned deep blue from bruising. He and his family moved from the house and tried to rent it to others who knew nothing of Sookie. This was the first and only night in the farmhouse for the new owner.

Over a period of time the new owner tried to rent the house to anyone who would stay in it. That did not work out very well. There was never a time when Sookie did not make her presence known. Eventually the new owner gave up trying to rent the house and just left it to sit on the property and fall into disrepair.

In the 1960s, Mr. Glover gained ownership of the property and began to farm the land. He completely disregarded the reputation of the land and old farmhouse. He mocked the idea of a dead woman being able to come back from the grave and control this land. He soon found out it was possible and costly.

Mr. Glover tried in vain to keep a hand pump by the old well to get water when he was working. He purchased several of them only to find them gone when the morning light brightened the new day. Once he tried staying overnight to catch the person who was stealing the pumps. During the course of the night, his attention was averted only once and that was just for a few seconds. When he looked again, the pump was gone, vanished as if in the thin air. As he looked in disbelief at where the pump once sat, he heard a low laugh from the back of his truck.

There have been things happen at the Sookie Field that Mr. Glover will not talk about. He purchased a new tractor for a great deal of money one season and almost did not get to leave the field before sunset. He climbed down from the tractor and left it running in the field. Remember this was a man who did not believe in the supernatural or any of its unearthly visitors. He will tell you now that it is unwise to be at Sookie Field after sunset.

When you ride down the road Sookie Field is located on, the closer you come to the house and the bridge where Sookie ended her life, the more you will feel that you are not alone. The presence of this being is malevolent and soon fear will creep deep into your very soul. It will stay with you until you have passed the house again on your way back. Maybe Sookie was right...this farm and everything about it is *still* hers and visitors are not welcome.

Chapter Nine:

CEMETERY GHOSTS

THE NATIONAL CEMETERY OF NEW BERN

(Craven County)

New Bern, North Carolina, is located in Craven County and has a population of approximately 29,000 people. It was originally a Swiss settlement and named after the capital of Switzerland, Bern. The city of New Bern also shares its flag. New Bern came to be by way of the Swiss connection of the English by Marian exiles and marriages of the royal house of Stuart. Many of these were people of importance in the history of Calvinism. Most people do not realize that it is also the birthplace of Pepsi Cola.

First settled in 1710, New Bern became a thriving community quickly. The Swiss and German immigrants who first came to live here were under the leadership of Franz Louis Michel and John Lawson. Christoph von Graffenried also played a major role in the guidance and leadership of the community. History tells us it was the permanent seat of the colonial government for North Carolina following the Revolutionary War and the first state capital.

In 1770, Tryon Palace was completed and became the home of British governor William Tryon. In 1815, New Bern boasted a population of 3,600 people. During the Civil War, New Bern was captured and occupied by Union forces.

Just a few miles from Tryon Palace you will find the National Cemetery. Several Confederate and Union soldiers are buried there, as are fallen soldiers from other wars. There are some graves in this cemetery that date back to the late 1500s and 1600s. Though their markers are all but gone, they still hold a certain fascination for those who come to visit. The National Cemetery is a beautiful and foreboding place all in the same breath. It conjures images of mystery and illusions of what or who may be close to you.

There is a high archway that gives entrance to the cemetery. Beyond this archway the massive old Oaks and Weeping Willow trees spread their cooling shade and add ever more to its mystic. There was a story about William Tryon that circulated for dozens of years that was in fact untrue. It was told by more than one person and passed down to generations that British governor William Tryon once dueled to the death at the archway of this cemetery. His shot went wide and the mark from the pistol ball striking the stone is still visible today. His adversary was true to his mark and struck William Tryon, wounding him. He died shortly after in Tryon Palace. Here it should be told that Governor Tryon was considered a good governor and died in his home in England in January 1787.

However, there *is* a pistol ball mark in the stone at the entrance, but its origin is unknown. Walk onto the paved path and you will discover many soldiers and civilians buried here and honored by the populace. It has the look and feel of an old cemetery that may be found in Europe and other foreign lands. It captures your every emotion as you walk past row upon row of loved ones lain to rest.

Witnesses have proclaimed seeing more than one apparition here and they swear to its validity. Near the southern corner of the cemetery, a witness told people close by that her boyfriend and two others were shading grave markers. This is the art of taking a large piece of paper and a stick of charcoal and tracing the wording on the headstone. They had been busy with their hobby about an hour when one of the people thought he had heard someone call his name. Thinking it was one of his friends, he asked what they wanted, but he quickly discovered that no one had called his name...as he was quite alone by the headstone. Minutes later he heard the voice calling him again. This time he decided to move to another portion of the cemetery.

Later in the afternoon the group gathered by the car to eat lunch and talk of the unique headstones and markers they had discovered while shading. The young man told of the voice calling his name.

Everyone laughed except for the other young lady in the group. She was unusually quiet and seemed a bit disturbed. She would never say she wanted to leave the cemetery and yet she would not re-enter the gates again when it came time to return. With the proper amount of prodding, she finally relented and told the little group what she had seen.

"I was walking toward one of the larger stones near the back of the cemetery. I stumbled over a small foot marker I didn't see and dropped my charcoal for the rubbings. When I bent over to pick it up, I caught something moving from the corner of my eye. I stood up and there was a woman with long grey hair and a dress that seemed to be from maybe the Civil War or longer standing close to the headstone I was going to. I felt scared because I knew she wasn't real. I wanted to run, but my legs didn't want to move. She smiled at me and then she seemed to almost melt into the headstone. I ran back over here and I am not going back over there today!"

The group decided it would be best to end their trip for the day, but vowed to return.

Sharing His Own Tale

As the author of this story, I had more than one experience here and will convey this to you. In the summer of 1978, I revisited National Cemetery. I wanted to continue investigating this cemetery based on the stories I was receiving from other people. The impressions I had received on the other occasions came back to me as if I had never left. It was a day that the shade of the trees was welcomed and I was able to get to a portion of the cemetery I had not been able to visit before.

I crossed over to the northeast side where there were some headstones that looked promising, for I am always interested in finding the oldest marker they have for my own curiosity. The moss covering the stones were like a step out of time. Delving ever deeper I found myself a little disoriented as to what part of the cemetery I was standing in. There was no sound anywhere for several moments. I did not hear any birds, or the scuffle of squirrels among the trees...*only dead silence*. Looking around me, I couldn't find my reference point for when I was to return, as there was nothing but headstones and foot markers.

I sat down by a broken marker and pulled my notes from my pocket and began to scribble on them. When my concentration was fully upon my notes and my surroundings deemed irrelevant, I felt a sharp tug on the sleeve of my shirt. I nearly fell over from the surprise of this as I thought I was alone — and I *was* alone! Looking around I could see no one, but the temperature had dropped dramatically where I was sitting. I reached down beside me, grabbed my hat, and, as suddenly as I bent over, my shirt was tugged on again, but this time close to my shoulder. I said nothing, but left hurriedly in a direction I had no idea as to where I would wind up.

The number of people who claim to have seen apparitions and heard voices are innumerable. A visit to the National Cemetery is well worth the trip.

A SHADOW BY THE GRAVE

(Hyde County)

Off the shores of Cape Hatteras is the island of Ocracoke. This island is also associated with the infamous pirate Blackbeard. Many pirates of the seas have set their sails for this island and bartered for goods and services throughout the island's history. The simplest way to reach this island now is to ferry from Cape Hatteras to Ocracoke. It is a thirty-minute ferry ride with the gentle winds of the sound against your skin as you drink in the natural beauty of all that surrounds you.

The beautiful waters of Ocracoke Island as the sun begins to set in the Carolina skies is a breathtaking view. These are the waters where the infamous Blackbeard and dozens of other pirates plied their trade and wars were fought for the freedom of the south.

The island is small, a mere twelve miles long, with white sandy beaches and pleasant residents to talk with while you relax. The underlying edge to the island is its long history and what lies beneath its sands. Just off Cemetery Road is the graveyard set in honor of British sailors who lost their lives during World War II off the coast of Ocracoke. Submarines of the German Navy lay in wait for unsuspecting merchant ships in the waters of the Atlantic, sinking as many as they possibly could. Thousands of lives were lost off these shores in World War II alone. The other ship battles that were fought off her shores date back to the 1600s. With these battles, the cannons roared like thunder and all but demolished the ships and crews they attacked. Those that weren't sunk were captured and looted for their cargo.

Some have stated the skull of Blackbeard is still held on this island and belongs to a secret society while others claim they hold the skull of the infamous pirate. If history is to be believed, the British claim his entire body, including his skull, was set about the four corners of London on pikes for all to see and know the penalty for piracy upon the high seas.

Close to the national cemetery for the British sailors are two other cemeteries of interest. These belong to the descendants of the island. Many are very old and the age of the gravesite is easy to discern with the markings on the headstones. Walking about the island, you will find the populace is contained in a relatively small area. Many homes of age are still inhabited by the same families that originally inhabited the island. A simple walking tour will take you to the lighthouse that is still operational and through the scrub trees that surround the village dotted with seaside homes. The roads all lead back to Cemetery Road and the shadow by the grave.

The summer of 1969 found Ocracoke still wondering if the next storm would be the worst they had seen. Bobby and his family had rented a small cottage on the island, which was located near one of the cemeteries on Ocracoke. He and his friends spent days on the beach swimming and laying in the sun. The white sands of the beach held a fascinating beauty with its contrast to the emerald blue waters lapping against the shore. Many nights he and his father fished from a small boat in the cool night air of the Sound. In the distance, they watched the ferry run forward and back, taking passengers to the island. The cemetery

At the rear of this cemetery, the unearthly shadow of a man hovered near the last headstone to the right.

could be seen from the waters they fished and Bobby kept finding himself drawn to its location. On the third night of their fishing, Bobby called his father's attention to the area of the cemetery. A faint light was moving slowly from one end of the graveyard to the other. Bobby and his father knew this was not possible for visitors were not welcome there, especially in the dead of night.

Bobby's father was a man of some morals. He did not feel it appropriate to disturb the sleep of the dead. He started the engine of the small craft and headed closer into shore for a better look. Getting as close in as possible, he was expecting to see the lights of a cottage more than the cemetery. He came in as close as he dared without taking the chance of damaging their boat. Picking up his binoculars he saw nothing out of the ordinary. The cemetery, or what he could see of it, was deserted. He laughed at himself for thinking otherwise. Bobby was not as easily convinced.

The next day Bobby told his friends what he had seen and convinced them to sit with him that night by the cemetery. Young boys have a fascination with the unknown. Their daring would not be equaled on this night. They came to the edge of the road and sat close by the cemetery watching the headstones intently. The hours passed and the boys succumbed to sleep. Bobby's father found them sleeping by the wooden gate and woke them. The boys were told to go home and stop their foolish vigil. Disappointed and a little afraid from being awakened so crudely, they headed for home.

Two days later Bobby's friends returned to the mainland and he was alone with his family on the island. Sitting by the cemetery gate for a brief rest, he looked back over his shoulder and saw the shadow of a man walking through at the rear of the cemetery. Jumping to his feet, his eyes followed the figure for a distance of fifteen feet straight into the trees. He was never able to see a man at all...only the distinctive shadow that walked silently across the sand. Bobby mustered all his courage. He knew in his heart he had finally seen a *real* ghost. Running to the back of the cemetery, to his dismay, there were no footprints in the sand. He had seen someone walk here and yet no footprints. He was elated that he had seen a ghost, but this feeling lasted only a very short time. His senses told him someone was very near and yet he could see no one. He looked everywhere and found nothing, but the feeling intensified. He soon felt as though something was reaching for him. Bobby ran the short distance back to the street and stared back at the headstones. The feeling of a presence was gone as if it had never been.

The last day of Bobby's stay upon the island seemed short. Wandering around, he found himself back at the gate of the little cemetery. Within minutes, he looked toward the rear of the cemetery and spotted a short stocky shadow of a man standing close by the tree. The shadow slightly turned to its left twice as if to leave and then turned back to face Bobby. It was not a dream and Bobby felt safe by the gate.

Within what seemed only a minute or two, the shadow moved from the tree crossing to the left of the cemetery. Bobby could see the headstones through the figure plainly. The shadow stopped once more by the headstone close to the end. It stayed by the headstone for an instant and slowly dissipated.

Bobby confided this story to his best friend and never told it again until he was much older and had children of his own. The shadow he spoke of never moved as if by deflection of the sunlight. It held all the attributes of a man and its actions were always that of a living person. There is the belief that the shadow had returned to the resting place of a loved one.

Other reports of this same small resting place have claimed the sighting of a middle-aged woman weeping by an old faded marker.

Chapter Ten:

THAT MYSTERIOUS WOMAN

A LADY IN BLUE

(Halifax County)

Halifax County, North Carolina, is a very unique area of the country. To visit historic Halifax one would only have to see the faces of the people who walk its streets and ply their trades to the public to feel the pride of their legacy. Halifax County came into being in 1758. It was annexed from Edgecombe County and named for the second Earl of Halifax, Charles Montagu Dunk, who was also the President of the Board of Trade and Plantations.

In 1758, a petition was put forth before the governor and the colonial assembly to change the status of this parish and make it an individual county. It had been a parish since 1741 and the county seat was aptly named Halifax. The original population of this area, which went all the way down to the southern banks of the Moratuck, which is now called the Roanoke River, was the Tuscarora Indians. They got along peacefully with the Europeans that came to settle here, but were soon removed from their homes and forced to relocate.

On April 12, 1776, the Fourth Provincial Congress adapted the Halifax Resolves during a meeting in Halifax. North Carolina became the first colony to take full independence from England, defying the orders of the British Crown. The years 1776 through 1782 were years of hard fought liberty for the men, women, and children of the state of North Carolina. It was here that nearly every session of the General Assembly was held and came the glory of Halifax.

The small town of Weldon is located in Halifax County. Its history intertwines with all of Halifax and its surroundings. The town literally sits almost beside the Roanoke River. This arena provided the means of trading, or selling, for everyone using the Roanoke River for commercial use. From the time of the Revolutionary War, it gained fame and prosperity. Famous men and women walked these streets and visited the homes of the very rich. Halifax residents, as well as Weldon residents, found themselves to be nearly one in the same for many years.

At the east end of town, close by the river, stands a beautiful building that has lately begun to be restored to its original splendor. It was reportedly built in the 1800s. This large brick building is one that presents itself with an air of dignity. Important meetings concerning the welfare of the people were held here as were social functions for the community. The years brought dozens of uses for a building that deserved never to be discarded for the sake of its age. Over one hundred years of service to its masters, this building has brought joy and wealth to many.

During the 1940s, one of its functions was as a place for high school dances for the surrounding community. On a cool September evening, Roger, his brother, and two friends decided to attend a dance that was to be held at this building. They had attended dances here before, but tonight was not to be just another dance! Roger was a young and daring man with a bit of temper and strength to match. His friends fell into the same league as Roger and the little band of men held no competition when it came to charming the ladies. They searched for young love and knew one day it would find them and life would be as it should. In a borrowed '38 Ford, they drove the short distance from Roanoke Rapids to Weldon and found themselves parked close by the banks of the Roanoke.

Roger remembered well getting out of the back seat of the car and hearing the music flowing from the open windows of the building. It almost seemed to reverberate back and forth off the banks of the river. They hurried to the open doors and entered the building, looking around to see if their favorites dates had been allowed to attend the dance. Standing to one side of the unlit fireplace, Roger found the young lady he had been looking for. He made his

This beautiful building is now under renovation to restore it to its past glory. It has been the scene of many hauntings through the years.

way through the small knot of dancers and stood close to the girl of his dreams. The evening was a success for all the young men and the happiness they felt worked deep into their hearts. They danced and laughed throughout the evening until close to 10 p.m.

In secluded corners, Roger had stolen kisses from his date and hoped he would be able to see her alone before the evening must end for them both. Working their way back over by the fireplace, he began to whisper lightly in her ear. She blushed, pushing him away gently. "Let's dance once more and then I will give you my answer." Feeling a bit dejected, he agreed and the two of them danced slowly to the romantic music filling the room.

There were approximately ten couples on the dance floor. Each couple held each other close and the world only turned for them. Just as the band began the chorus of the love song, a long figure emerged from just beyond the fireplace in a very elegant baby blue ball gown. She seemed to be a lady of prominence from days long gone. She held her head high and proud as she lifted one slim

This is the room where a young man and many of his friends first saw the apparition of a beautiful woman dressed in a blue ball gown.

While photographing this building, two energy orbs in the left second floor window were captured. There was nobody in the building and nothing to reflect light from this area. Note the orbs are on the inside of the window behind the wood and glass. These orbs are in the same room as the men reported seeing the lady in the ball gown.

ghostly white hand...as if she was accepting the hand of an unseen partner. Roger and several of the other dancers saw her almost at once. He stood fascinated by the fact you could see the far wall and the fireplace right through her. Before he could react, the lady was already waltzing through the small crowd and heading for the open double doors. It happened very quickly almost in a breath of time. Roger and his date asked everyone they knew if they saw the lady in the blue dress. Several said they had, but they also said this was not her first visit to a school dance.

For the next several years the lady in the blue ball gown appeared to those within the walls of this fine building. Whether it was a dance or a meeting of some importance, she would be seen almost waltzing across the room from the fireplace to the double doors that exit the building.

Roger joined the Marine Corps some years later and served his country in the Korean War. Whenever he passed this building, he would tell the tale of the lady in the blue ball gown. He was never able to find out the name of the ghost and his eyes filled with longing to know more of her. In the words of a man who has seen this vision of the past, "She was the most beautiful woman I have ever seen."

DOWN BY THE SEA

(Dare County)

The Outer Banks of North Carolina hold a certain fascination in the lives of everyone who come to visit. It is a place of wonder for its natural beauty and the simple pleasures of life. The abundance of wildlife and its bountiful fishing areas provide pleasures to delight even the simplest of demands. Thousands come to visit these shores yearly and most always return.

History, drama, war, and talented artisans can all be found from Currituck to Ocracoke Island. Each town or community you visit here is sure to welcome you. The clear southern skies over the islands offer a symphony of heavenly beauty that is rarely equaled. Sit upon the white sandy beaches by the warmth of a glowing campfire and tales of the unknown surround you.

This is the base of the Cape Hatteras Lighthouse as it stands today. It was moved from its original location in 1999. No reports of anything unusual or spirits returning to the lighthouse have been reported since then.

There is a very special place along this chain of barrier islands that visitors from afar come just to walk its beaches and see a magnificent structure that has stood the test of time for over one hundred years. It is the Cape Hatteras Lighthouse, and could very well be one of the most famous lighthouses in the world today. The sands of time nearly ran out for her in 1999 when she had to be moved to her present location, 175 yards down the beach toward Ocracoke Island. Severe beach erosion had beaten a path nearly to her door threatening her destruction. Thanks to all of the citizens around the country, they were able to raise the millions of dollars needed to

have her moved further down the beach and safe from the ravages of the Atlantic Ocean.

The lighthouse was built in 1870 and required 1,250,000 baked bricks to erect this masterpiece of engineering. Weighing 6,250 tons, she stands on a floating foundation of heart pine. Cape Hatteras Lighthouse stands nearly 208 feet high from her base to the top...where the view of the Outer Banks is something you will never forget. She holds the distinction of being the tallest lighthouse in the nation.

Through hurricanes and tropical storms, she has stood bravely on the shore of this barrier island and never failed in her duties. Her light shining out to sea for twenty miles has kept hundreds of ships — from schooners to the heavy ships of the United States Navy — off the Diamond Shoals and sure disaster.

Families have spent much of their lives by this lighthouse with frequent gatherings and special celebrations. Some come to just sit beneath her shade and drink in the serenity of its location while others come to within sight of the lighthouse to go fishing on the beaches that surround her. At certain times of the year, fishing tournaments for Puppy Drum made the lighthouse a flurry of activity.

Time does not stand still for this lighthouse. Pleasant memories that last forever have been created here. Young couples have come to the Cape Hatteras Lighthouse to be wed. The words of their vows and of a never-ending love echo through the sounds made by the surf washing against the shores of the beaches here. Some say it's just the wind. Others can almost swear it is the voices of those long past. Either way, it is for you to decide.

No one knows where the young woman wearing a dress of white came from, nor do they know her name. Her dress is simple with puffed sleeves and a nondescript piece of jewelry pinned to the ruffled collar close to her elegant neck. So young and pretty, she walks near the stone steps leading to the entrance of the Cape Hatteras Lighthouse. Witnesses say she hesitates and looks about her as if someone is long overdue to meet her. The lady gives the appearance of having medium brown hair worn tightly in a bun at the back of her head. This is hard to distinguish because the parts of her body that are supposed to be flesh are shadowy and indistinct. It is then that you realize this young lady is standing on thin air! You can see the brickwork of the lighthouse through her as she stands waiting...for someone who never comes. Her visits have been reported to occur close to dusk when the last rays of the Carolina sun are lighting your way. She fades away slowly, leaving one to wonder if their senses are not playing tricks on them.

The date of the first sighting of this young lady is not known. However, Mr. Midgett passed this tale to me at the age of 73. He stated he had first witnessed her apparition when he was just a small boy. He and his father had taken the journey from Kitty Hawk to Hatteras Village to work for a man who lived there. Mr. Midgett had never been allowed to accompany his father on work assignments that far from home before, but his father deemed it was time he became a man and learn his father's trade.

Mr. Midgett had seen the Cape Hatteras Lighthouse from the waterside many times and it always gave him wonder how a man could build a structure of this size. To a small boy nothing could ever surpass what he had seen. His eyes gazed in wonder at the lighthouse as they passed within her shadow, and his amazement grew with every step they took. He dared not ask his father to stop so he could get closer, but he knew in his heart he would see her in her glory that very night. He did not have long to wait. They reached their destination and gathered their things to sleep out on the beach. Father and son built a small fire and cooked their dinner by the sea. Mr. Midgett remembered well the smell of the salt air and the gentle breeze from the ocean that caressed his face that night. It was as if he had finally become a man in his father's eyes. They talked as men talked and watched the light from the lighthouse as it shone brightly into the night over the waters of the Atlantic. Mr. Midgett dreamed of the wonderful life that lay ahead for him.

Father and son worked for their employer for three days. The work was hard, but not difficult. Mr. Midgett learned everything he could from his father and listened well to everything he had to say. At the end of the third day, his father said he could go and visit the lighthouse, but not to stay too long and meet him back by the camp. They would sleep on the beach again that night and leave for home at sunrise.

Just as the last rays of sun began to fade Mr. Midgett had left the base of the lighthouse and stood back from its steps for one last look before leaving. He craned his neck trying to see the top of the lighthouse, but he was too close and had to move further away. Just as he was about thirty yards from the lighthouse, something caught his attention near the stone steps. The hair on his neck began to rise as he watched a young woman in a long white dress gradually appear before him. He said nothing as he watched her glide to a place close to the entrance steps leading inside the lighthouse.

He could feel more than see that she was unhappy. Mr. Midgett tried, in vain, to get a clear look at her face and could not. Still he could not seem to find his voice to speak to her. It was as if she were shrouded in a mist of fog. She turned slightly from him in an attempt to leave where she stood, but this was not to be. As quickly and quietly as she had appeared, she faded before his eyes.

Mr. Midgett ran from the lighthouse, never looking back. He ran back along the beach through the deep sand, finally reaching his father's camp and collapsed. He sat patiently waiting for his father's return and wondered if what he had seen was real.

Looking up the beach he saw his father walking towards him with a small smile on his face. After a good fire was built and they had eaten their supper, he praised his son for the fine work he had done and gave him a ten-dollar gold piece. Mr. Midgett was elated. He had never seen that kind of money in his entire life. His father said the man they worked for gave them a bonus for a fine job and finishing before the deadline. Mr. Midgett was so excited he could hardly speak, and yet what he had seen earlier would not stop plaguing his young thoughts. It was written on his face like the carving of stone.

His father knew well that something was bothering his son and wanted to get to the bottom of it. He wasted no time and asked him why he was so upset. His father sat and listened as the boy told him what had happened at the lighthouse. At the end of his story, his father's reaction was not what he had expected. His father explained calmly that there were things in life that a man could see and still could not be explained, but not to worry. He continued on to say he also had seen the lady he was talking about. He told Mr. Midgett that on his tenth wedding anniversary he and Mr. Midgett's mother saw her while they were walking back from the beachhead. They had been walking in the moonlight when they encountered her and she was glowing in the dark like a white Saint Elmo's fire.

They talked more about the things nature and God produced well into the night. The rest of his life he remembered the words from his father on that night by the firelight and heeded them well. He passed the wisdom on to his children as well. Mr. Midgett smiled a tiny smile and said, "I guess I may owe her something for making me what I am today. If I had not seen her, the possibility of me and my father talking that night may not have happened."

The sighting of this lady in white was always at the original placement of the lighthouse. You may wonder if she will go with the lighthouse after it has been moved.

Chapter Eleven:

WATERY GHOSTS

OUT OF THE MIST

(Hertford County)

The mighty Chowan River merges with the Black and Nottaway rivers at the North Carolina/Virginia state line. It then winds its way east for fifty miles to enter into the Albemarle Sound. It is said to be the most beautiful river in the world. The Chowan River flows through swamplands while passing little high ground. Drifting down this magnificent waterway the Cyprus trees line the shores on both sides of the river, creating a portrait that could only be reproduced by nature itself. The land behind these trees is filled with Oaks, Hickory, Ashe, tall Long leaf pines, and varieties of Dogwood. Scuppernong grape vines grow wild along these shores.

In the years before and after the settlers began arriving, the Meherrin Indians and other tribes indigenous to the area lived off the land here. Its abundance of wildlife and natural fruit trees made life much easier than early settlers expected.

The Indians knew of many unearthly beings that inhabited these woods as well as the river itself. Their tales could be heard around any campfire as well as the surrounding towns and villages. The Tuscarora Indians told a tale that has spread through history about an Indian princess who had fallen in love with a warrior from another tribe. The young girl's father denied their love and the union was not meant to be. There are as many as five variations of this story. They all have the same account as far as after the young woman lost her life. Some say she committed suicide. Other accounts say she drowned. In either case, they all claim to see the same thing. The witnesses claimed to see a white canoe crossing the river with a beautiful ghostly Indian maiden paddling slowly toward the shore only to disappear before their eyes.

The validity of the story has lost its value for many for the simple reason it is the same story, but in a different location. There are those who have never seen a beautiful Indian maiden, but their story bears witness to what they did see. In the early 1950s, a young Hertford County man and his father-in-law decided to go fishing on the Chowan River. They rose early and drove to a boat landing on the Gates County side of the river. They had fished together many times before and were familiar with each other's methods of catching fish.

The sun was just beginning to show itself against a Carolina blue sky when they left the mouth of the creek and started toward a small island noted for an Eagles nest. After taking a good look at the height of the tide and a quick survey of the wind, they decided to take themselves on the lee side of the island until the wind died down. A half-mile from the island they could see a slight mist riding lightly on the surface of the water. They came into the creek side as slowly as possible to reduce the possibility of striking a hidden log or other objects floating in the water. All about them the mist wafted through the Cyprus trees, not unlike clouds in a dream.

The two men fished these waters for a couple of hours, nearly filling the fish coolers they had brought with them. The smile on their faces could not be contained. They knew this was unusual luck, but they were not going to make a second guess as to why they were so lucky.

By 7 o'clock on that fine morning, they cranked the motor of the small wooden boat and moved away from the lee side of the island. They moved up river about one hundred yards to the Hertford County side to a fish hurdle they had built the year before. As the young man turned off the motor, his father-in-law dropped the anchor over the port side of the boat. The sound of the rope dragging over the gunwale echoed ever so slightly across the river. The father-in-law tied off the anchor and reached for his favorite fishing pole.

When he lifted his head, he noticed his son-in-law was standing in the boat, staring down the river where they had just been fishing. Without turning, he said, "We can go back up there before it gets too hot and catch a few more fish before we go home. I was wanting to see if the White Perch were in here yet."

The young man responded in a questioning tone of voice as he noted, "I didn't see anybody else around the island when we were up there, but I can see somebody now."

The old man turned around just in time to see someone paddling away from the lee side of the island through the mist. The old man laughed lightly. "Whoever it is, he is gonna have a time paddlin' against that tide."

They watched the small craft emerge from the mist and continued with ease to the Hertford County side of the river. He paddled effortlessly and gained momentum with each stroke of the paddle. Barely before he reached the cover of the huge Cyprus trees, he faded from their sight.

Both men were well aware that he did not have time to reach shore and they were also well aware that there was no place to land a boat in that area. The old man looked closely at his son-in-law. "I ain't had a drink this morning and I know you didn't either. So you tell me what I just seen coming from the island."

The young man studied for a second and responded like a man in a bad dream. "I don't know about you, but I could swear I just saw an Indian in one of them old style canoes come cross the river like it was nothin'. I know an Indian when I see one and he looked like an old fella to me. What I cain't quite get through my head is, I could see the Cyprus trees right through him. If I didn't know better, I would swear I just saw a ghost."

The old man nodded his agreement and they dropped the subject for the time being. The rest of the morning was a fishing disaster. Not another fish was caught and the water of a river that usually moved steadily was still as the surface of a lake. After a few more hours of fishing in all of their favorites places with no luck, they packed up and headed for home.

The following day was Sunday. This was the day the family all came over to visit and play music. The old man sat back in his rock-

The man in the canoe was first seen paddling from the mouth of this creek across the main waters of the Chowan River.

ing chair on the front porch as they played all their favorite gospel songs. The girls sang and the men tapped their feet to the beat of the music. Eventually the musical instruments were laid to rest against the house and the men sat talking at one end of the porch with the women on the other end. The talk worked its way around to fishing stories. The old man sat back and chuckled, "We saw somethin' yesterday I would have never believed if I hadn't seen it. Now I'll tell you what it was and if you doubt my word you can ask him." With this, he pointed at his son-in-law and then relayed the story just as they had experienced it.

A good friend of the family spoke up quickly after he had finished his story. "I believe you. Joe Taylor has seen the same thing for years. He fishes at night and tries to get back home for breakfast and then head for the shipyard. He ain't the only one either. I can give you a hand full of folks that have even chased that canoe and never caught it. Everybody says you can look right through him. It disappears up by the Cyprus trees and that ends it. The thing is, if you are like the rest of the folks that has seen the old Indian, you left something out of your story. You caught a lot of fish before you seen him, and after he came by, you didn't get nothing'."

The old man nodded in agreement. The tale of the old Indian still passes through the family from father to son. There may be a time when you can enjoy fishing on the Chowan River. Just remember, when you fish around the island in the wee hours of the morning, ask yourself, 'Are we alone?'

Two men watched as a phantom canoe paddled against a hard current with ease and then disappeared into the Cyprus trees at this point of the river.

A DIAMOND SHOALS GHOST

(Hyde County)

Diamond Shoals is well known for being one of the most treacherous bodies of water in the world. It lies off the shores of the barrier islands of the coast of North Carolina. The location of shipwrecks here run from Cape Henry to Cape Lookout and number in the hundreds. Over a century of time, the number of men, women, and children who have lost their lives in these waters is staggering. It has a beauty all its own that nature has never reproduced anywhere. To stand on her shores and watch the sea mist mix with heavy rains while the white caps pound the beaches is something a man could never forget. It is a land of endless time.

This is a land where hard-working men earned their living fishing the sea. Each day brought new challenges for them as well as new dangers. From as far back as the old men can tell their tales, there have been shipwrecks here. The pirates and wreckers plied their trades here, and the wars along this stretch of water date back well into the 1600s. The ships fought each other for money and power with the price once again being life lost.

The wreckers were not all bad men like the pirates. Some of the wreckers did their bidding out of survival and tried to save anyone still aboard the wrecked ships. Other wreckers would leave their victims to die as they stood on the decks of their ships, not caring about their plight. All of the wreckers lured the ships to shore by hanging a lantern about the neck of a nag and walking him down the beach. This gave the ship's captains the impression they were farther from shore than they were. The schooners and other ships sailed close in and ran aground on the shoals, to be torn apart by the pounding surf and prevailing harsh winds of the Atlantic. The wreckers came in and took anything and everything of value for themselves and often times retained salvage rights for what was left of the ships. The authorities soon became wise to their scheme and wreckers became another matter for history books and fireside tales.

There have been cases where the wreckers actually lured in the ships and brought the passengers and crew into their homes to stay with them while they went back to the ships and plundered the cargo and whatever was left of the rigging and iron works.

Nor'easters and hurricanes ravage these shores, overwhelming everything in sight...especially ships. The heavy winds and raging seas drive the ships ashore and tear them to pieces. It is not uncommon for Captains who have wrecked to tell authorities he was already aground before he ever saw the shore. It is with little wonder than that this area has been aptly named Graveyard of the Atlantic.

A true mystery to all is a magnificent schooner built in 1919 in Bath, Maine. The *Carroll A Deering* was a five-masted schooner that sailed the seas with pride. On January 29, 1921, her captain and crew had the *Carroll A Deering* before the wind, making sail on a return trip from Barbados to Hampton Roads, Virginia. She passed the Cape Lookout Lightship easily enough, but the lighthouse keeper reported later that the crew "just seemed to be milling about on the deck." There was also a crewman who did not look or act like a ship's officer. The lighthouse keeper made note that the *Deering* was missing her anchors. Another ship also spotted her. It was the *SS Lake Elon*, which was sailing southwest of the Diamond Shoals Lightship. This sighting had taken place at approximately 5:45 in the afternoon.

The captain of this vessel reported that the *Carroll A Deering* looked to be steering a peculiar course. Lightship Captain Thomas Jacobson remembered well when he stood upon his quarterdeck and was hailed by a man from the *Carroll A Deering*. It was very unusual for the entire crew to be standing on deck. The man who hailed the lightship captain did not look, act, or speak like a ship's officer. The crewman shouted they had lost their anchors riding out a gale south of Cape Fear, which is located near Wilmington, North Carolina. The man also requested they notify the Deering company of their plight. This being said, the *Carroll A Deering* sailed silently out of sight, making its way along the coast.

Jacobson tried to contact a steamer passing by to relay the message because his radio was not working aboard the lightship. This was to no avail because the steamer passed them completely ignoring a signal from them. Jacobson was unable to see a name for the steamer. It was maritime law at this time that a ship responds to the

Along the shores of the Cape Hatteras lay ship wrecks by the hundreds. This is the site of the final resting place for the *Carroll A Deering*, which was mysteriously abandoned and left to be ravaged by the wind and the waters of North Carolina's Diamond Shoals.

whistle of a lightship. The steamer made no effort to respond or even slow its speed.

This was the final report of the *Deering* until approximately 6:30 in the morning of the 31st of January. C. P. Brady of the Lifesaving Station at Cape Hatteras spotted a five-masted schooner in the first light of day run hard aground and helpless on the shoals. She was seen with all sails set and her decks flooded with seawater. No sign of life was to be found on her decks and her lifeboats were missing. The heavy seas proved to be too much for rescuers from the life saving station and she could not be boarded until 9:30 a.m. on the morning of February 4th.

The men from the lifesaving station of Cape Hatteras boarded the ship only to find no one onboard to explain what had happened to the *Deering*. Important papers from the Captain's quarters were missing, and navigational equipment and charts were also not found. Food in preparation for a meal was found completely intact. It was discovered that others than just the Captain had been sleeping in the Captain's quarters before she was wrecked.

The matter was set into investigation by President Herbert Hoover. His team of investigators was able to unearth clues leading to the destruction of the *Deering* and many leads were directed at mutiny by the crew. The final findings on the case of the ghost ship *Carroll A Deering* was anything but ordinary. The evidence did not fit when it came to mutiny, nor was there any finding to conclude that piracy was ever involved.

Captain Balance of the Cape Hatteras Station believed the crew took everything of value and abandoned her to wreck upon the shoals intentionally. If this is true, the question arises as to why no one saw her for an entire day before she was found aground on the shoals. Then there is a matter of the ship's log, navigational equipment, and the disappearance of an entire crew. The intensive government investigation never came up with any evidence as to what happened to the *Carroll A Deering*, the ruins of which still lie just below the sand on the beaches of Cape Hatteras. She remains to this day a true ghost ship.

INDEX